C. S. LEWIS' TOP TEN
INFLUENTIAL BOOKS AND AUTHORS

WILL VAUS

C. S. Lewis' Top Ten:
Influential Books and Authors, Vol. 1

Copyright © 2014 Will Vaus

Winged Lion Press
Hamden, CT

All rights reserved. Except in the case of quotations embodied in critical articles or reviews, no part of this book may be reproduced or transmitted in any form or by any means, electronic or mechanical, including photocopying, recording, or by any information storage or retrieval system, without written permission of the publisher.
For information, contact Winged Lion Press www.WingedLionPress.com

Winged Lion Press titles may be purchased for business or promotional use or special sales.

C. S. Lewis portrait on title page by Robyn Hannaman is used by permission of the artist and The Edwin W. Brown Collection at Taylor University.

10-9-8-7-6-5-4-3-2-1

ISBN 13 978-1-935688-08-2

**In memory of
Christopher Mitchell**

Contents

C.S. Lewis and Friends Study Center Book Series		1
Introduction		3
I	*Phantastes* by George MacDonald	9
	Lewis' Reading of MacDonald	9
	MacDonald's Life	20
	Book Synopsis	26
II	*The Everlasting Man* by G.K. Chesterton	45
	Lewis' Reading of Chesterton	45
	Chesterton's Life	47
	Book Synopsis	58
III	*The Aeneid* by Virgil	81
	Lewis' Reading of Virgil	81
	Virgil's Life	87
	Book Synopsis	93
Conclusion		125
Acknowledgements		131
Endnotes		133
Bibliography		157
Index		161
Winged Lion Press Backlist		168

C. S. Lewis & Friends Book Series

With the cooperation of Winged Lion Press, the Center for the Study of C. S. Lewis and Friends at Taylor University plans to publish one volume of distinguished scholarship every two years. *C. S. Lewis' Top Ten Influential Books and Authors, Vol. 1* is the third book in this series. Our interest centers on work concerning C. S. Lewis, George MacDonald, Dorothy L. Sayers, Owen Barfield, and Charles Williams. Authors with book-length manuscripts who would like their work considered for future volumes may send a cover letter and proposal to Program Director / Center for the Study of C. S. Lewis and Friends / Taylor University / Upland, IN 46989. http://library.taylor.edu/cslewis/index.shtml

The Center for the Study of C. S. Lewis & Friends is housed at Taylor University in Upland, Indiana, located in the Midwest of the U.S.A. With a mission to promote the kingdom of God through the study of exemplary Christian authors, the Center serves the Taylor University campus, the local community, and a worldwide academic and lay audience. We offer several programs to reach these various groups. For our students, we hold classes on the works of C. S. Lewis and several related authors—primarily, but not exclusively, George MacDonald, Dorothy L. Sayers, Charles Williams, and Owen Barfield. For our local community, we present regular C. S. Lewis Society Meetings, featuring lectures and discussions on the works of Lewis and related authors. And for our more distant friends, we organize the biennial Frances White Ewbank Colloquium on C. S. Lewis & Friends, which gathers scholars and readers from across the United States and around the world. For all of these groups, we maintain one of the finest rare book and manuscript collections, which we have named after its collector, Edwin W. Brown.

The Edwin W. Brown Collection includes first English and American editions of books authored, edited, or with prefaces by C. S. Lewis, published essays and lectures of Lewis, several Lewis letters, and two Lewis manuscripts ("Light" and *Clivi Hamiltonis Summae Metaphysics Contra Anthroposophos Libri II*). The collection also contains books about C. S. Lewis, as well as first and reprint editions of Charles Williams, Dorothy L. Sayers, George MacDonald, and Owen Barfield. Individuals or groups interested in visiting the collection are welcome during the academic year, when we hold regular hours; special arrangements can also be made for other times. We are always eager to share our collection with new friends.

INTRODUCTION

Clive Staples "Jack" Lewis (1898-1963) was the author of over thirty books, ranging from literary criticism to the Narnia tales for children, from science fiction to popular theology. Lewis has been called the bestselling Christian author of all time with over 200 million copies of his books in print. He has also been cited as one of the most oft-quoted spokespersons for Christianity, second only to Jesus of Nazareth and the Apostle Paul.[1]

Scholars have been trying to answer for decades: "What has made C. S. Lewis such a great writer with so large a following?" One answer to that question which has yet to be fully explored is Lewis' vast and deep reading across the entire canon of Western literature, from Homer and the Bible down to some of the most important works of the early twentieth century.[2] It seems to me self-evident that before one can become a great writer one must be a great reader. Most certainly, C. S. Lewis was a voracious consumer of books.

In 1962, *The Christian Century* magazine asked Lewis: "What books did most to shape your vocational attitude and your philosophy of life?"[3] *The Christian Century* posed this question to a number of writers across a broad spectrum, asking them to list up to ten books excluding the Bible (since most Westerners would naturally include the Bible on such a list of influential books). In response, Lewis offered the following list:

1. *Phantastes* by George MacDonald
2. *The Everlasting Man* by G. K. Chesterton
3. *The Aeneid* by Virgil
4. *The Temple* by George Herbert
5. *The Prelude* by William Wordsworth
6. *The Idea of the Holy* by Rudolf Otto
7. *The Consolation of Philosophy* by Boethius
8. *Life of Samuel Johnson* by James Boswell
9. *Descent into Hell* by Charles Williams
10. *Theism and Humanism* by Arthur James Balfour

Given a reading life as rich as that of C. S. Lewis, the man probably had a hard time paring down his list to the *top ten* books that influenced him. An adequate account of *all* of Lewis' literary influences would require numerous thick volumes.[4] However, Lewis' top ten list provides a good place to start our examination of the reading that made him one of the greatest writers of the twentieth century. Furthermore, limiting the scope of our research in this way means that we can begin to cover the territory in the space of three thin volumes, instead of an untold number of thick ones.

Each chapter in this volume will be divided into three sections:

1. An overview of Lewis' reading of the author.
2. A thumbnail biography of the author.
3. A synopsis of the particular book.

In the course of each chapter, I will point out particular ways that the author and book may have influenced Lewis as well as, in some cases, similarities between Lewis' life and that of the author.

Now, right at the beginning, I must state a qualification. I am not an expert on any of the top ten books or authors that Lewis named in his response to *The Christian Century*, though I am somewhat of an expert on Lewis and his work. "So why write a book like this at all?" you might well ask. Lewis has already answered that question perfectly for me in his introduction to *Reflections on the Psalms*. There he writes,

> I write for the unlearned about things in which I am unlearned myself. If an excuse is needed (and perhaps it is) for writing such a book, my excuse would be something like this. It often happens that two schoolboys can solve difficulties in their work for one another better than the master can. When you took the problem to a master, as we all remember, he was very likely to explain what you understood already, to add a great deal of information which you didn't want, and say nothing at all about the thing that was puzzling you. I have watched this from both sides of the net; for when, as a teacher myself, I have tried to answer questions brought me by pupils, I have sometimes, after a minute, seen that expression settle down on their faces which assured me that they were suffering exactly the same frustration which I had suffered from my own teachers. The fellow-pupil can help more than the master because he knows less. The difficulty we want him to explain is one he has recently met. The expert met it so long ago that he has forgotten. He sees the whole subject, by now, in such a different light that he cannot conceive what is really troubling the pupil; he sees a dozen other difficulties which ought to be troubling him but aren't.[5]

Therefore, in this book, as Lewis says somewhere, I am like "one inky fourth former" suggesting to another inky fourth former how to get on. However, before we dive into the main content of this volume, I believe something more should be said about Lewis' reading life in general.

A lifetime devoted to reading began for C. S. Lewis in his childhood home. In his autobiography, he tells us that both his parents were "bookish" people and that their home was filled with a seemingly endless number of books, some suitable for children and some not, but none were forbidden him.[6] Lewis was home-schooled until the age of ten, learning French and Latin from his mother and "everything else from an excellent governess".[7] By the age of eight, Lewis was reading such books as: Arthur Conan Doyle's *Sir Nigel*, Twain's *Connecticut Yankee in King Arthur's Court*, E. Nesbit's children's books, Swift's *Gulliver's Travels* and Beatrix Potter.[8] Before age ten, he read Milton's *Paradise Lost* for the first time, even jotting down some notes thereon.[9]

Lewis' own childhood paradise was lost when the security of his comfortable home was shattered by his mother Flora's death from cancer in 1908. Lewis' father Albert almost immediately packed Jack and his elder brother Warren ("Warnie") off to boarding school in England. Under the tutelage of a sadistic headmaster, Lewis' education languished for two years. However, the boy continued to read on his own, among other things: *Quo Vadis, Darkness and Dawn, The Gladiators, Ben Hur*, Rider Haggard and H. G. Wells.[10] Mercifully, Lewis' boarding school in Watford, Hertfordshire, was shut down in 1910 and Lewis' father sent him briefly to Campbell College, Belfast. At Campbell Lewis read for the first time Matthew Arnold's poem *Sohrab and Rustum*. His imagination was immediately captured by the "silvery coolness, a delightful quality of distance and calm, a grave melancholy". Already, by the age of twelve, Lewis' literary experiences were becoming the most important events of his life.[11]

Halfway through his first and only term at Campbell, Lewis fell ill and was sent home. His father, dissatisfied with the school, decided to send young Jack off to Great Malvern, England, where Warnie was a student at Malvern College. Jack was sent to Cherbourg Preparatory School in the same town. It was there that Jack "ceased to be a Christian" partly through the influence of the school Matron but also because of his wide reading. In reading Virgil, in particular, Jack encountered a mass of religious ideas that his teachers took to be false. However, no one took the time to explain to him *why* they thought all other religions to be nonsense and *why* Christianity just happened to be true.[12]

Around the same time that Lewis gave up his Christian faith, he also fell in love with Norse mythology. Then, in the library of Malvern College, during the 1913-1914 school year, he added to Norse a growing affection for Celtic and Greek mythology as well. To his knowledge of French and Latin Lewis was adding studies in Greek. Under the tutelage of Harry Wakelyn Smith, the classics master at the college, Lewis was especially learning to enjoy Horace's *Odes*, Virgil's *Aeneid* and Euripides' *Bacchae*.[13]

Despite the joys introduced to Lewis' life by the college library, the "Gurney", and his classics master, "Smewgy", Lewis was not happy at school. For one thing, he did not like "games", and life at Malvern College was seemingly dominated by athletics. The other hardship was the "fagging" system in which younger boys, like Lewis, were required to perform menial chores, such as shining shoes, for upper classmen. As a result, Lewis was tired as a cab horse for much of his time at the college. He repeatedly requested that his father find him some other means of preparation for life at university; in the end Albert relented.[14] In the autumn of 1914, Jack was sent to the same tutor in Surrey who had so admirably prepared his elder brother Warren for the entrance examination to Sandhurst Military Academy.

Lewis arrived at Great Bookham on a Saturday in September. At nine o'clock on Monday morning Lewis sat down with his tutor, William Kirkpatrick, to begin work on Homer. Kirkpatrick, or "The Great Knock" as the Lewis family called him, read aloud the first twenty lines of the *Iliad*. He then translated about a hundred lines. When he had finished, he handed Lewis a Greek lexicon and told him to go through as much as he could of what he had done. At first, Lewis could travel only a short distance along the trail The Great Knock had blazed. Soon he journeyed further; eventually he was able to go beyond the distance of his tutor's translation on his own. Before he left his tutor for Oxford, Lewis had learned French, Italian and German in the same manner.

Obviously, Homer wasn't Lewis' only reading at Great Bookham. There was also Demosthenes, Cicero, Lucretius, Catullus, Tacitus, Herodotus, Virgil, Euripides, Sophocles, and Aeschylus. On top of his reading in the classics, Lewis read various authors in the other languages he was learning. He also read a great variety of British authors for his own pleasure: Austen, Blackwood,[15] Boswell, Bridges, the Brontës, Coleridge, Herrick, Hewlett, Keats, Lang, Mackail, Malory, Mandeville, Milton, Morris, Peacock, Ruskin, Scott, Shakespeare, Shelley, Sidney, Spenser, Swinburne, Walton, and above all—Yeats.[16]

On 7 April 1916, Kirkpatrick wrote the following to Albert Lewis about his son:

> He has read more classics than any boy I ever had—or indeed I might add than any I ever heard of, unless it be an Addison or Landor or Macaulay. These are people we read of, but I have never met any.[17]

It is quite amazing in a way, given the breadth and depth of the young C. S. Lewis' reading, that there was one author, a Victorian novelist and author of mythic tales, who would come to tower above all the rest in Lewis' mind and imagination. It was while living with his tutor in Great Bookham that Lewis happened upon a work of this well-known author for the first time, a volume Lewis would later name as the number one book that most influenced his vocation and philosophy of life. . . .

PHANTASTES BY GEORGE MACDONALD

Lewis' Reading of MacDonald

In his autobiography, *Surprised by Joy*, published in 1955, C. S. Lewis recalled his first encounter with the work of George MacDonald.[18] The year was 1916 and Lewis was in the habit of walking from his tutor's home in Great Bookham, Surrey, to Leatherhead about once a week and then taking the train back, a distance of three to four miles each way. On one of these journeys, Lewis picked out for his weekend reading an Everyman copy of *Phantastes* from the railway station bookstall.[19] That evening he started into the book. MacDonald's tale of a woodland journey, ghostly enemies, and ladies fair, was similar in many ways to other stories Lewis enjoyed. Thus, he was drawn into the book without realizing there was something different about this story. It was a long while before Lewis was able to give a name to this new quality that he encountered in *Phantastes*, but eventually he realized that the "bright shadow" resting on the travels of the hero Anodos, was the shadow of holiness.[20]

For the first time the song of the sirens that Lewis had heard in other mythic tales sounded like the voice of his mother or perhaps his childhood nurse. The golden light of MacDonald's story cast a shadow of "Joy", not only over Lewis' reading, but also over his everyday life. "Joy" was almost a technical term in Lewis' parlance, referring to an experience of intense longing, desire, or what the Germans called "sehnsucht". The light of MacDonald's new country made all of Lewis' erotic and magical perversions of "Joy" look sordid in the brightness of day.[21] However, at the same time, the reading of *Phantastes* caused Lewis to look at ordinary things, like bread on the table or coals in the grate, with an entirely new appreciation. As Lewis later said, the first night he read *Phantastes* his imagination was baptized.[22]

Three days after he purchased *Phantastes* Lewis wrote in his weekly letter to his Belfast friend, Arthur Greeves, about the great literary experience that had occurred in his life. Lewis shared with his friend that he had just discovered another author to add to their mutual circle of favorites. One of Lewis' beloved authors at that time was William Morris; Lewis especially enjoyed Morris' tale, *The Well at the World's End*.[23] Lewis told Arthur he felt MacDonald was as good as Morris, or even Sir Thomas Malory, author of *Le Morte D'Arthur*; Lewis urged his friend to purchase *Phantastes* at once.

Lewis despaired of trying to adequately describe *Phantastes* to Arthur.

Instead, he invited his friend to follow the hero of the story, Anodos, along the little stream to the fairy wood, to hear of the terrible ash tree, and read about the fairy palace. It is quite clear that the very atmosphere of MacDonald's faerie romance had cast a spell on the young Lewis.

Nonetheless, Lewis' literary critical faculties were still wide-awake from his very first reading of MacDonald. He urged Arthur not to be disappointed with the first chapter of *Phantastes*; Lewis rated it as very conventional fairy tale style. Furthermore, he warned his friend that MacDonald's poetry, with one or two exceptions, was very poor. However, despite these drawbacks, from the first Lewis considered MacDonald a genius.[24]

By the time Lewis wrote again to Greeves, on 14 March, he was asking for his friend's verdict on the book. By the 21st, he learned that Greeves enjoyed the story, though Arthur only began to like it by the eleventh chapter. Lewis was disappointed at this for he felt that the best chapters were the ones dealing with the forest scene and the fairy palace. He hoped that Greeves had by this time purchased MacDonald's *Sir Gibbie* and would be advising him about it. Lewis found even the titles of some of MacDonald's books most alluring, such as *At the Back of the North Wind*.[25]

Lewis told Greeves that he was familiar with the feeling of being on the brink of some wonderful happening in his life. This feeling came very much because of his reading of MacDonald. It was not hard for him to imagine himself as part of MacDonald's story. He asked Arthur what he would do if confronted by the ash tree, or if he found his house melting into a haunted wood. Wouldn't he long for this dull world again? Lewis coined a new term to describe the type of world he was discovering in MacDonald. He called it "Terreauty", a combination of terror and beauty. He thought that perhaps just such a world was indeed being offered to him every day if only he had the courage to step into it. Thoughts such as these were floating through Lewis' mind, not only because of his reading of MacDonald, but because, as he told Arthur, he had been reading Maeterlinck, to improve his French, and that rather too late at night.[26]

By 16 May, Lewis was looking forward to Greeves' comments on *At the Back of the North Wind*[27] and by 4 July, Lewis and Greeves were both writing their own stories, borrowing consciously or unconsciously, from *Phantastes*.[28] Later that same month Lewis was reading *Letters from Hell*, a book with introduction by MacDonald.[29] Lewis' reading of this book may have planted in his mind the idea that eventually germinated in the writing of his own *Screwtape Letters* many years later.

By the end of 1916, Lewis had read MacDonald's fairy tales.[30] On 15 November, he wrote to Greeves expressing his surprise because his friend did not say more about MacDonald's *Golden Key*. To Lewis, that book was "absolute heaven". One wonders what influence, direct or indirect, MacDonald's fairy tales had on the writing of Lewis' Narnia books.³¹

There is no further mention of MacDonald in Lewis' letters until October 1919. At that time Lewis happened to mention that he was reading MacDonald's poems in bookshops, being too poor to purchase the books and take them home.³²

For an account of Lewis' state of mind as an Oxford undergraduate we must turn, once again, to his autobiography, written almost thirty years after the fact. In *Surprised by Joy*, Lewis talks about the time-period when he was reading for his degree in English literature from 1922 to 1923. He says that all the books he was reading at that time were beginning to turn against him. That is to say, his reading was making it harder and harder for him to remain an atheist. He notes, in particular, that George MacDonald had done more *to him* than any other writer; but at the time, Lewis thought it a pity that MacDonald was a Christian. He felt a similar ambivalence toward Chesterton and Johnson, two authors we will examine further. Even among classical authors, Lewis found it was the religious ones who really "fed" his soul; that is, if he had a soul; he still wasn't sure. Lewis mentions Plato, Aeschylus and Virgil, as his three favorite classical authors. On the other hand, authors with whom Lewis felt he ought to have some sympathy, people like Shaw, Wells, Mill, Gibbon and Voltaire, all seemed a bit shallow. The attraction Lewis felt "most alarming of all" from the standpoint of his atheism, was the feeling he had for the work of George Herbert. Lewis felt that Herbert was better than anyone he had ever read at conveying the quality of real life, but Herbert insisted on mediating that quality through what Lewis then called "Christian mythology". The only non-Christian authors with whom Lewis had any sympathy in the early 1920s were the Romantics,³³ but even some of their writings were tinged with religion, and even Christianity.³⁴

According to Lewis' diary, in January 1923 he was re-reading *Phantastes*, which by then he had read many times. Significantly, he said it filled for him the place of a devotional book.³⁵

There is no further mention of MacDonald in Lewis' letters or in his diary until his journal entry of 19 August 1925. While on holiday in Exmoor with his "adopted mother", Mrs. Janie King Moore, Lewis decided to order by mail MacDonald's *Lilith*. Interestingly enough, while on holiday Lewis found that the only authors he could read were MacDonald and Wordsworth.³⁶ On August 21, Lewis received a card from the bookstore informing him that *Lilith* was out of print.³⁷ Still Lewis persisted and eventually got hold of a copy. By 15 June 1926, he must have read *Lilith*, because he mentions it in his diary entry for that day. That morning Lewis woke up early from "an abominable dream" apparently inspired by the "life in death of the poem in MacDonald's

Lilith."[38] Despite the nightmare, by 24 June, Lewis was re-reading the book.[39]

1926 was an important year in C. S. Lewis' own career as an author. It was in that year, on September 20[40] to be exact, that he had his second book published, an epic poem entitled *Dymer*. Lewis' biographer and friend, George Sayer, has pointed out that Dymer's quest is the same as that of Anodos in *Phantastes*. Both seek the eternal feminine.[41]

We don't hear of MacDonald again, in Lewis' correspondence, until he writes to Arthur Greeves on 10 October 1929. By this time, according to Lewis' autobiography, a great change has taken place in his life, for in the Trinity Term of 1929, that is, in the spring, he kneels in his room at Magdalen College, Oxford, and admits that God is God. He was, he tells us later, perhaps the most dejected and reluctant convert in all England.[42] Given his return to theism, Lewis' reading at this time should come as no surprise. Yet, at the time it was a surprise to Lewis himself. In his October letter to Arthur, he tells his friend that he is slowly reading a book that they both have known about for a long time—MacDonald's *Diary of an Old Soul*. Lewis almost chuckles to himself at the thought of how he would have scorned such a book at one time.[43] He strongly advises Greeves to read it. This in itself is amazing, for Greeves was, at one time, urging Lewis to embrace Christianity, but now Lewis is recommending a devotional book to Greeves. Lewis comments that MacDonald seems to know everything and that he, Lewis, finds his own experience reflected constantly in *The Diary of an Old Soul*. Lewis is even coming to the point of liking MacDonald's literary "clumsiness". He finds in MacDonald's poems a delicious homespun, earthy flavor, similar to that in the poetry of George Herbert. Amazingly, Lewis declares to Greeves that for him, MacDonald is better than Herbert.[44] Lewis continued to read daily from *The Diary of an Old Soul* during this period.[45]

The homespun quality of MacDonald's work, or what Lewis sometimes called "homeliness", was indeed very important. In fact, Greeves was the one who first led Lewis to enjoy this quality, not only in literature, but also in nature and everyday life. In October 1929, Lewis recorded in a letter to Greeves the comment of another friend, Owen Barfield, which is very much relevant to this point. Barfield noted to Lewis that the idea of the spiritual world as our *home* and the discovery of "homeliness" in that which is otherwise remote—was a literary quality peculiar to certain British authors. Barfield felt that MacDonald, Chesterton, and his friend Lewis had this quality in their writing more than anyone else.[46] It is rather interesting that Barfield would include Lewis in the same category with MacDonald and Chesterton at this early date since Lewis, at the time, only had two published works of poetry to his credit.

On 27 February 1930, in another letter to Arthur Greeves, Lewis expresses his continuing change of heart towards MacDonald's literary faults, declaring that they are "obvious" but that they don't seem to matter.[47] Then in his letter of 7 June to Greeves, for the first time Lewis recognizes the quality of holiness inherent in MacDonald's work.[48]

By this time, Greeves, being more financially well off than Lewis, had acquired quite a large collection of MacDonald's works. Lewis told Greeves how much he envied him and longed to look over the MacDonalds with his friend's guidance.[49] Lewis further noted that he had read both *The Princess and the Goblin* and *The Princess and Curdie*. In fact, he had read the former for about the third time when he was ill in the spring of 1930. Lewis especially noted for Arthur's attention the passage in *The Princess and the Goblin* where Curdie, in a dream, keeps on dreaming that he has awoken but finds he is still in bed. Lewis points out to Greeves the connection between this passage and another in MacDonald's *Lilith* where Adam says to Lilith, "Unless you unclose your hand you will never die and therefore never wake. *You may think you have died and even that you have risen again*: but both will be a dream." Lewis then draws the parallel to the spiritual life, especially his own. It is far too easy, Lewis says, for imaginative people like himself to think that because they enjoy the idea of certain spiritual efforts, therefore they have achieved them. However, this is not the case. (At this time, Lewis was desperately trying to obey his conscience but failing on an almost daily basis.[50]) Lewis tells his friend he is appalled to see how much of the spiritual and moral change that he thought he had undergone recently was only imaginary. The real work was, yet, remaining to be accomplished.[51]

Lewis realized his main problem was that he needed to die to self, but that it was impossible for him to do so on his own power. He wrote to Greeves about this on 18 August.[52] While not achieving for him this spiritual death, Lewis found his continued reading of MacDonald to be providing for him a great feeling of spiritual cleansing and healing.

In August 1930, Lewis read MacDonald's novel, *Wilfrid Cumbermede*, while sitting naked under the willows at Parson's Pleasure, one of his favorite swimming locations in Oxford.[53] He concluded that MacDonald's novels "have great and almost intolerable faults" and that the only literary form in which MacDonald excelled was that of fantasy like *Phantastes* or *Lilith*.[54] Nonetheless, Lewis noted how certain themes in his own epic poem, *Dymer*, published in 1926, were borrowed from MacDonald.[55] Lewis thought *Sir Gibbie*[56] to be the best of MacDonald's novels he had read up to this point in time, though he planned to read *Wilfrid Cumbermede* again.[57]

On 15 September 1930, Lewis clarified for Greeves his thoughts on MacDonald's novelistic technique. What Lewis decried was the fact that the most valuable kind of story, the *Phantastes* kind, was constantly being interrupted in MacDonald's novels by an inferior type of story.⁵⁸

Apparently, Greeves did not agree with Lewis on this point. Thus, Lewis wrote to his friend on 29 October saying that they must agree to disagree. What Greeves found to be the exciting part of the story in *Wilfrid Cumbermede*, Lewis found to be "a pure drag". However, certain parts of *Sir Gibbie* seemed to Lewis much better because the excitement in it was that which he considered to be: "the *real* sort", and not interrupted by the mere machinery of the old melodramatic three-volume novel.

Lewis informed Arthur that he had recently bought two other MacDonald novels: *Adela Cathcart* and *What's Mine's Mine*. The first Lewis thought "definitely bad" and he felt the same way, incidentally, about *The Seaboard Parish*. Lewis recognized the quality of holiness in both novels but he felt it degenerated into "mere flat moralizing" by the end. When reading MacDonald's novels he thought it sometimes hard to even realize he was reading the same author who wrote *Phantastes*.⁵⁹

This is not to say that Lewis completely disliked MacDonald's novels. On 24 December 1930 he wrote to Greeves saying that *Annals of a Quiet Neighbourhood* went far to restore his faith in MacDonald as an author. One reason why Lewis enjoyed this particular novel so much was that he read it immediately after Trollope's *Belton Estate*. Lewis enjoyed reading Trollope throughout his life, especially when ill in bed. However, on this occasion Lewis felt like he was constantly making excuses for Trollope on the moral side. Upon turning to MacDonald, a writer of the same period, Lewis was astonished at the difference in moral quality and felt "ashamed to have spent even an hour in a world so inferior as that of Trollope's".⁶⁰

However, after reading *Alec Forbes*, Lewis was down in the dumps again. He felt nothing but rage at the tragedy of MacDonald being forced to write novels for money, thus being diverted from writing the fantasies which were his true area of literary talent.⁶¹ Strikingly, Lewis thought this literary loss to be as great as the early death of Keats.⁶²

Despite this blow, Lewis was soon on the upswing of the MacDonald reading rollercoaster. On 17 January 1931, he wrote to Greeves about *What's Mine's Mine*. He rated this novel just below *Phantastes*, *Lilith*, MacDonald's fairy tales, and *The Diary of an Old Soul*. Lewis admitted that the novel subordinates story to doctrine. However, Lewis found MacDonald's "preaching" in the novel to be of such a high quality that he planned to re-read the book many times.⁶³

We read little of MacDonald in Lewis' letters again until his momentous letter of September 1931 where he tells Greeves of his important talk with his friends Hugo Dyson and J. R. R. Tolkien, a conversation which leads, in short order, to Lewis' return to Christian faith. In this same letter, Lewis mentions that the MacDonald conception of death (really St Paul's idea) is the answer to William Morris. Lewis says that if ever he feels that his book and pipe and chair are enough to provide true happiness it only takes a page or two of Morris to sting him with uncontrollable longing for something more. All Morris does, notes Lewis, is to rouse the desire: but so strongly that the reader *must* find the real satisfaction.[64]

Lewis returns to this idea in his next letter, the one in which he announces to his friend Greeves his return to Christian faith. Lewis notes that he has just finished reading St Paul's letter to The Church at Rome, the first Pauline letter he ever seriously read through as an adult. He admits that *Romans* "contains many difficult and some horrible things"[65] but the essential idea of Death (the MacDonald idea) is there, and that is the most important thing. Lewis explains to Greeves how this idea answers to the hunger for a country where no one dies, as in William Morris' *Earthly Paradise*.[66]

After his return to Christian faith in 1931, Lewis' letters often refer to George MacDonald and his work. Naturally, MacDonald continued to be a topic of conversation in his letters to Arthur.[67] However, we also see references to MacDonald, and quotes from his works, in Lewis' letters to his brother Warren, Owen Barfield, Sheldon Vanauken, and numerous other correspondents.[68]

In a letter to Arthur written on February 4, 1933, Lewis mentions how Tolkien is another friend who, like them, grew up on William Morris and MacDonald.[69] In the same letter, Lewis mentions the curiosity of supervising a young, female student who is writing a thesis on MacDonald. For Lewis, it felt strange having to deal with MacDonald from an academic perspective after having so long enjoyed a more intimate, personal acquaintance with MacDonald's work.[70]

Lewis often recommended MacDonald's books to various correspondents, and even instructed them in how to obtain second-hand copies of volumes long out of print.[71] In his first letter to the Anglican nun, Sister Penelope, on 9 August 1939, he asks her if she is familiar with "MacDonald's fantasies for grown-ups".[72] Lewis also recommended MacDonald's fairy tales to children who enjoyed his own Narnia books.[73]

In a letter written on 26 March 1940, Lewis recommends MacDonald's *Unspoken Sermons* to a former student, Mary Neylan.[74] It is obvious from reading this letter and others from Lewis' pen, that he continued to read MacDonald after his return to Christian faith in 1931 and he obtained great spiritual nourishment especially from reading MacDonald's three volumes of *Unspoken Sermons*.[75]

In 1946, Lewis published an anthology of quotations from George MacDonald.[76] The quotations are taken largely from the *Unspoken Sermons* as well as some of MacDonald's other works.[77] Many of the quotes from MacDonald echo or anticipate Lewis' thoughts on various topics. For example, quote #1 about "Dryness" from MacDonald is "That man is perfect in faith who can come to God in the utter dearth of his feelings and desires, without a glow or an aspiration, with the weight of low thoughts, failures, neglects, and wandering forgetfulness, and say to Him, 'Thou art my refuge'." This sounds very much like this statement from Screwtape: "Our cause is never more in danger than when a human, no longer desiring, but still intending, to do our Enemy's will, looks round upon a universe from which every trace of Him seems to have vanished, and asks why he has been forsaken, and still obeys."[78]

Entry #10 in the MacDonald anthology about "The Word" reads thus: "But herein is the Bible itself greatly wronged. It nowhere lays claim to be regarded as *the* Word, *the* Way, *the* Truth. The Bible leads us to Jesus, the inexhaustible, the ever unfolding Revelation of God. It is Christ 'in whom are hid all the treasures of wisdom and knowledge,' not the Bible, save as leading to Him." Lewis obviously came to hold the same view of the Bible, influenced by MacDonald and others, no doubt. In a letter to a Mrs. Johnson, written on 8 November 1952 Lewis says: "It is Christ Himself, not the Bible, who is the true word of God. The Bible, read in the right spirit and with the guidance of good teachers will bring us to Him."[79] Lewis writes about his view of Scripture in greater detail in *Reflections on the Psalms*.[80]

Then, in Entry #322 on "Prayer" in the MacDonald anthology we read, "But every honest cry, even if sent into the deaf ear of an idol, passes on to the ears of the unknown God, the heart of the unknown Father." In the same letter, quoted above, to Mrs. Johnson, Lewis says: "I think that every prayer which is sincerely made even to a false god or to a v. imperfectly conceived true God, is accepted by the true God and that Christ saves many who do not think they know Him. For he is (dimly) present in the *good* side of the inferior teachers they follow."[81] Lewis pictures this concept in the character of Emeth in *The Last Battle*.[82]

George MacDonald: An Anthology was dedicated to Lewis' former student, Mary Neylan, who had taken a great liking to the works of MacDonald thanks to the recommendation of her former tutor. In the Preface to the *Anthology* Lewis notes that he has never concealed the fact that he considered MacDonald his master. He fancies that he never wrote a book in which he did not quote from him.[83] We have seen three examples of this from the *Anthology* itself. To fully flesh out the truth of Lewis' claim would require a book unto itself. However, I think a few more examples of Lewis "quoting" MacDonald, beyond those already provided from the *Anthology*, are in order.

In *The Screwtape Letters*, Screwtape mentions how he detests both music and silence.[84] The inspiration for this line came from MacDonald's

Unspoken Sermons, First Series, 'The Hands of the Father,' pp. 187-188, where MacDonald says,

> Nor shall we ever know that repose in the Father's hands, that rest of the Holy Sepulchre, which the Lord knew when the agony of death was over, when the storm of the world died away behind his retiring spirit, and he entered the regions where there is only life, and therefore all that is not music is silence, (for all noise comes of the conflict of Life and Death).[85]

Lewis refers to MacDonald in a chapter entitled "Counting the Cost" in *Mere Christianity*. He develops an illustration taken from an idea expressed in one of MacDonald's novels. Lewis points out how every father is pleased at his child's first attempt to walk, but no father is satisfied with a son or daughter continuing to walk like a baby through his or her adult life. This idea is taken from MacDonald's novel, *Donal Grant*, chapter 42, where he says of God: "Easy to please is he—hard indeed to satisfy."[86]

Lewis refers to MacDonald again a bit later on in the same chapter. Here he utilizes MacDonald's illustration of imagining one's life as a house. God comes in to rebuild the house of one's life and we may think, at first, that we understand what God is doing. However, after awhile, God starts knocking our house about in a way that hurts terribly and doesn't seem to make any sense. The reason it doesn't make sense is that God is building a different house than what we imagined in the first place. Rather than fashioning us into nice little cottages, God is making us into castles in which he is going to come and live.[87]

Of course, the C. S. Lewis book in which George MacDonald figures most prominently is *The Great Divorce*. In this slim volume, published in 1945, MacDonald acts as Lewis' guide to the afterlife in a similar manner to Virgil acting as guide to Dante in *The Divine Comedy*. In some ways, Lewis uses this device to rehabilitate some of the theological ideas of MacDonald, such as the limited nature of hell.[88]

MacDonald's book, *The Miracles of Our Lord*, clearly influenced what Lewis wrote in his own volume, *Miracles*.[89] Lewis underlined many passages in MacDonald's book. Two of the most significant are these:

> This, I think, is the true nature of the miracles, an epitome of God's processes in nature beheld in immediate connection with their source.[90]

> So long as they regard only the surface of them, they will, most likely, see in them only a violation of the laws of nature: when they behold the heart of them, they will recognize there at least a possible fulfillment of her deepest laws.[91]

Furthermore, what MacDonald wrote in his volume, *Dish of Orts*, certainly influenced Lewis' own ideas on imagination. This volume in Lewis' library is heavily annotated. Lewis kept a running summary of MacDonald's main points in the first chapter on "Imagination: Its Functions and Its Culture" and the last chapter on "The Fantastic Imagination". Lewis underlined the following significant passages in *Dish of Orts*:

> But while the imagination of man has thus the divine function of putting thought into form, it has a duty altogether human, which is paramount to that function—the duty, namely, which springs from his immediate relation to the Father, that of following and finding out the divine imagination in whose image it was made.[92]

> In physical things a man may invent; in moral things he must obey— and take their laws with him into his invented world as well.[93]

> A fairytale is not an allegory. There may be allegory in it, but it is not an allegory. He must be an artist indeed who can, in any mode, produce a strict allegory that is not a weariness to the spirit.[94]

There is little doubt that Lewis kept on recommending the theological thinking of his literary mentor right up to the end of his life. Lewis quotes MacDonald in his essay *The World's Last Night*, first published in 1952. In that essay, Lewis talks about the folly of trying to predict when Christ will return. He notes that George MacDonald has written well of this folly and quotes MacDonald:

> Do those who say, Lo here or lo there are the signs of his coming, think to be too keen for him and spy his approach? When he tells them to watch lest he find them neglecting their work, they stare this way and that, and watch lest he should succeed in coming like a thief! Obedience is the one key of life.[95]

After compiling his George MacDonald anthology, Lewis was invited on a few occasions to write further about MacDonald. However, in each case he turned down the opportunity. In response to an invitation from Clyde Kilby to provide a Preface for a new edition of *Phantastes*, Lewis maintained that he had already said all that he had to say about MacDonald and his work. On another occasion, when asked to write a monograph about MacDonald and his books, Lewis at first responded with some enthusiasm, but then begged off. He thought the writing of such a volume would require more effort than he would be able to give to such a project.[96]

Some of Lewis' many correspondents, becoming aware of his love for George MacDonald's books, offered to send him copies in the mail. In one instance, Lewis turned down a first edition of *Phantastes*, saying that he would not be the proper owner for such a book. This was due, Lewis said, to his age, and the fact that soon after it was given to him, the book might need to find a new home. Lewis suggested that the correspondent give the book to the library of MacDonald's old college in Aberdeen, Scotland.[97] On another occasion, Lewis accepted a gift of MacDonald's three-volume novel, *Malcolm*, because he did not have that work in his library; perhaps he was willing to accept the gift because it was not a first edition.[98]

At the end of his life, Lewis invited a number of close friends to choose a single volume each, from his library, as a sort of remembrance of their friendship. When it came time for Lewis' former student, friend, and later biographer, George Sayer, to choose a book, he asked if he might have George MacDonald's *Unspoken Sermons*. Lewis very quietly objected saying, "Well, that's three volumes." Sayer very politely chose another book instead.[99] Even as he was approaching death's door, Lewis found it difficult to part with the books written by his greatest literary mentor; they had become like old friends.

MacDonald's Life[100]

George MacDonald was born in Huntly, Aberdeenshire, Scotland on 10 December 1824. Two years later, his family moved to "The Farm" on the outskirts of Huntly. Today, the house is known as "Greenkirtle". It is the home where MacDonald was raised. Helen MacKay, George MacDonald's mother, died of tuberculosis in 1832. George was just eight years old. C. S. Lewis, in similar fashion, lost his mother to cancer when he was nine years old. Both men were deeply affected by these early losses. However, unlike Lewis, MacDonald gained a loving stepmother in 1839. Amazingly, she outlived her stepson by five years.

George's father, George MacDonald, Sr., was a faithful member and deacon of the local independent chapel. C. S. Lewis mistakenly refers in one of his letters to George MacDonald as a Presbyterian, but such was not the case. MacDonald's grandmother, Isobel, was responsible for introducing the family to the dissenting church. Grandmother MacDonald "combined an extremely severe demeanor with a great capacity for love."[101] The faith of his father and grandmother had a profound impact on the young MacDonald who took churchgoing very seriously. However, young George reacted strongly against some of the tenets of the Calvinism prevalent at that time. When he heard about the doctrine of election he said that he did not wish God to love him if God did not love everyone.[102]

In 1840, at the tender age of sixteen, George MacDonald entered King's College, Aberdeen, an institution very much imbued with the Calvinist perspective. At King's, MacDonald received a Christian humanist education along with heavy doses of Reformed theology. Sundays were exclusively devoted to rest, worship and study, the latter being focused upon the Heidelberg Catechism. During his years at King's, George was most interested in the sciences, receiving quite good grades in chemistry and physics. However, limited finances prevented him from pursuing his desire for medical studies. Therefore, his focus turned to another interest—literature—especially fairy tales. Through reading the German Romantics, especially Novalis, during these years, MacDonald was exposed to a Christian spirit that provided a delight and a counterpoint to Calvinism. In the end, George received a Master of Arts degree from King's in 1845.

Although he wanted to return to his family farm, George's delicate health dictated otherwise. In addition, his college studies had well prepared him for the life of a teacher. Having served as a tutor of younger children during a year off from college, he decided, for the moment, to continue work in a similar vein. George's father had a friend in London, the Reverend John Morrison, who was able to place George as the tutor of some children in a wealthy family who were members of his nonconformist congregation.

George's strong interest in the Christian faith led him to continue his studies at Highbury Theological College in London in the autumn of 1848. At the same time, MacDonald kept abreast of developments in the scientific world. Among other things, he read about Darwin with great interest and openness to his ideas. Many years later, Lewis would demonstrate a similar perspective, espousing in books such as *The Problem of Pain* a theistic evolutionist outlook.[103]

On the denominational question, MacDonald was becoming increasingly nonsectarian. "I would rather be of no sect than a sectarian," he said.[104] In this, too, we see a foreshadowing of C. S. Lewis and "mere Christianity".[105] MacDonald was determined to figure out what he believed for himself, based upon the Bible alone, and especially on the Gospels.

Through his cousin, Helen MacKay, MacDonald was introduced to the family of James Powell, an upper middle class evangelical who had a thriving business in the leather trade. Helen married Powell's son, Alexander, in 1844. MacDonald soon became interested in one of Powell's six daughters, Louisa. In 1848, George asked this small and humble girl, with beautiful blue eyes, two years his senior, to marry him.

During his years at Highbury seminary, MacDonald was influenced by John Godwin, principal and professor of theology and New Testament. Godwin's orthodoxy was sometimes questioned, for Godwin was an Arminian in the midst of Calvinists. A much greater influence on MacDonald was Alexander John Scott, Chair of English Language and Literature at University College, London. MacDonald attended Scott's lectures during his seminary days and was keenly interested, not only in what Scott had to say about literature, but in the man himself. Scott was a former Presbyterian who had his preaching license revoked due to his objections regarding the Presbyterian doctrines of election and the Sabbath.

In 1850, MacDonald accepted a call to serve as pastor of the Trinity Congregational Church in Arundel, Sussex. He was ordained the following year and found himself sufficiently situated financially to marry Louisa.

The task of preparing a sermon every week was overwhelming to MacDonald, at first. He much preferred to be writing poetry. Still, he persevered in his pastoral duties. In addition to Sunday sermons, there was a Monday night prayer meeting and a Thursday evening lecture in which he expanded upon the sermon from the previous Sunday. Amidst all of these duties, MacDonald still found time to write poetry, and even to translate the work of the German poet, Novalis, into English.

It wasn't long, however, before some members of the Arundel church found fault with the preaching of their new pastor. They found many of his sermons to be far too pointed with practical application, but how could they object to that? Instead, they voiced their complaints about MacDonald's theological liberalism. They sensed that his teaching on the universal presence of sacramental grace was out of accord with the general teaching of Congregationalism. MacDonald was, perhaps, still finding his way, theologically. However, he came to the point where he firmly believed that no person would be condemned to hell that had not had sufficient opportunity to decide for or against Christ. He came to believe that all people would be given such a clear opportunity after death. He also held out hope that the animal kingdom would experience redemption. On these two points, C. S. Lewis would find much agreement with his literary mentor.[106]

As a result of MacDonald's pointed, practical preaching and his unorthodox views, the movers and shakers in the Trinity Church voted to reduce their pastor's salary hoping that this would encourage him to move on elsewhere. As Lewis pointed out in the Preface to his anthology of MacDonald, the members of the Arundel church had misjudged their man.[107] MacDonald chose to stay on at the church and make do, despite the fact that his family now included his first child, Lilia Scott.

Eventually, however, the situation became intolerable; MacDonald resigned as pastor in 1853 and moved to Manchester where he lived with his brother Charles. Since MacDonald had no means, at first, to support his family, Louisa, now with two children to care for, was forced to live with her brother Alec and his wife Helen in Liverpool. MacDonald scraped by financially by providing irregular pulpit supply for various Congregational churches. George and Louisa were eventually reunited but then were faced with a further trial, when George experienced hemorrhaging from the lungs. He eventually recovered, and took to lecturing out of his home both on physics and literature. Through these endeavors, along with occasional tutoring, George was able to support his family.

However, lecturing and tutoring weren't MacDonald's only activities at this time. He continued writing poetry. His first book, *Within and Without: A Dramatic Poem*, was published in 1855. It did not take long for MacDonald's work to capture the attention of Britain's literati. In 1856, Lady Byron, widow of the poet Lord Byron, became MacDonald's first patron. When MacDonald's health suffered during that same year, Lady Byron and other wealthy friends made it possible for MacDonald and his wife, with their daughter Mary who was also unwell, to take an extended holiday in Algiers while their other children stayed in England with relatives. They hoped that the warmer climate would help to heal George's lungs. In Algiers, MacDonald continued to demonstrate his broad, ecumenical convictions by attending Roman Catholic Mass. He was also fascinated by the worship of the Muslims whom he encountered there for the first time.

In 1857, MacDonald and family returned from Africa and settled into a home they called Huntly Cottage, located in the southern English town of Hastings. The following year was a momentous one for MacDonald. He published the book that would eventually have a marked influence on the life of C. S. Lewis, *Phantastes*. However, sadly, during the same year MacDonald lost both his brother John and his beloved father.

Still, by 1859, life began to look up for MacDonald. He accepted the professorship of English literature at Bedford College, London and eventually moved his family there. Through Lady Byron, MacDonald was introduced to various people in London literary circles. However, one of MacDonald's closest friendships of this period was with a man to whom he was introduced by his doctor. The man's name was Charles Dodgson, who, under the pen name of Lewis Carroll, and with the encouragement of the MacDonald family, would eventually publish *Alice's Adventures in Wonderland*.

MacDonald wanted to continue writing but felt at a loss about what to write. *Phantastes* had not sold well and so his publisher had encouraged him to consider writing a novel. MacDonald made an unsuccessful first attempt and concluded he could never become a novelist. However, his father's death provided inspiration for a character mirroring his father's own Scotch sternness combined with a remarkable tenderness. The character was David Elginbrod and the novel of the same name was published in 1863.

In 1865, MacDonald continued lecturing, but now his teaching was conducted at King's College, London. The following year he became a member of the Church of England at the Chapel of St Peter, Vere Street, where his theological and spiritual mentor, F. D. Maurice, was the Rector. By this time, the MacDonald family had grown substantially. In 1867, George MacKay, the last of eleven children was born to George and Louisa. That same year the family was able to move to a larger home. They dubbed the house "The Retreat"; it was located in Upper Mall, Hammersmith, in the western part of London. In 1867, MacDonald also had published the first of his series of *Unspoken Sermons*.

In addition to lecturing and writing books, MacDonald became involved with the housing projects for the poor of London started by his friends, John Ruskin and Octavia Hill. MacDonald would often go to the renovated slum projects to talk to people about Christ. The poor of London were welcome at The Retreat as well, where many were attracted by Louisa's first attempts at putting on various family enacted theatrical productions.

Many of MacDonald's novels were first serialized in magazines. One of these periodicals was called *Good Words for the Young*. MacDonald became the editor in 1869. One of his well-known fantasies for children, *At the Back of the North Wind*, was published in 1871.

In addition to fairy tales, MacDonald continued to publish many novels. However, his strongest interest in writing was simply to communicate the love of Christ to his readers. Thus, he also undertook to publish more directly theological works like *The Miracles of Our Lord*, published in 1870. MacDonald took the position that miracles do not violate or suspend the laws of nature. Rather, miracles demonstrate an acceleration of God's working through nature. C. S. Lewis later expressed this same view in his book, *Miracles*.

MacDonald's novels were popular not only in Great Britain but "across the pond" in America. Thus, in 1872, George, Louisa and their son, Greville, went on a lecture tour across the United States. While in America the MacDonalds spent time with some of the literary greats of the era such as Mark Twain. In addition, in the year of their visit to the United States, MacDonald had published another fairy tale for children entitled *The Princess and the Goblin*.

In the 1870s, Louisa began to organize family performances of *Pilgrim's Progress*. Princess Louise attended one of these productions. Perhaps as a result, Queen Victoria awarded to George MacDonald a Civil Lists Pension in 1877, yielding one hundred pounds annually.

However, not all was well with the MacDonald family in 1877. George and Louisa's daughter Mary was having severe health difficulties due to an advanced case of consumption. Therefore, the family chose to leave England and spend some extended time in Italy where they hoped the warm weather would help Mary's physical state to improve.[108] Sadly, Mary died of tuberculosis in 1878. She was buried at Nervi. The next year, tragedy struck again. MacDonald's son Maurice died. To make matters worse, as a non-Catholic, Maurice was denied burial in the local Catholic cemetery and therefore his body had to be interred on a rocky hillside. Overwhelmed by grief, MacDonald tried to soldier on, even seeing another novel, *Sir Gibbie*, through to publication in 1879.

After living in various rented accommodations in Italy for some time, the MacDonalds were eventually, with the help of wealthy friends, able to have a home built to their specifications in Bordighera. As always, they gave the house a name; this time it was *Casa Coraggio*. The family settled into their new home in 1880, the same year that MacDonald's *Diary of an Old Soul* was published. Writing the book had helped MacDonald to cope with the deaths of Mary and Maurice, just as, many years later, writing *A Grief Observed* would help C. S. Lewis to cope with the death of his beloved wife, Joy Davidman.

In Italy, the MacDonalds continued to open their home to all whom the Lord brought to them. Week by week MacDonald even offered teaching, both on English literature and the Bible, to small groups that would gather inside *Casa Coraggio*. During these years, he also continued to write and publish. *The Princess and Curdie*, *The Gifts of the Child Christ*, and *A Dish of Orts* all appeared in 1882. The latter was a collection of essays. In one of the essays, MacDonald expressed his view that the human standard for imagination is to be found in God. Rolland Hein summarizes MacDonald's perspective in this way: "All of nature, which is constantly being created by God, is a result of God's imaginative thinking."[109] The idea of God continuing to create in the present, rather than having finished his creation in the past, was another belief Lewis shared with MacDonald.[110]

While life in Italy helped to sustain George MacDonald in better health than he had experienced in England, the same cannot be said for his children. The MacDonald family continued to suffer great loss. Daughter Grace died in 1884, and Lily in 1891. However, as with the death of his father, and Mary and Maurice, so also the deaths of MacDonald's daughters brought inspiration through suffering. The result was, perhaps, his greatest work of fantasy, entitled *Lilith*. It was published in 1895. In the ensuing years, MacDonald continued to write and publish. However, now over 70 years old, the visionary gleam declined after the publication of *Lilith*.

In 1901, Louisa and George celebrated their golden wedding anniversary. Sadly, Louisa died the following year and was buried in the Stranger's Cemetery in Bordighera, beside the bodies of Grace and Lily. George MacDonald spent the last five years of his life in almost complete silence, unable to speak. He died on September 18, 1905 in Ashtead, Surrey. His ashes were later interred in his wife's grave in Bordighera.

Phantastes: A Synopsis

The book begins with a quotation, as does each chapter. It should not be surprising that one of the first quotes is from one of MacDonald's great literary influences, Novalis. "One can imagine stories without rational cohesion and yet filled with associations, like dreams."[111] This quotation well sums up the nature of *Phantastes*, a dreamlike book with, at times, little cohesion. Perhaps this is why C. S. Lewis had a hard time describing the book to his friend Arthur Greeves. The reader discovers after completing a first reading of *Phantastes* that it is like waking from a dream.[112] One remembers snatches, but the whole of it quickly fades away. However, here is an attempt to bring the whole back to the forefront of memory . . . .

Chapter I—The Fairy in the Cupboard
The hero, Anodos,[113] on his twenty-first birthday, is entrusted with the keys to his dead father's secretary desk. Opening the desk, Anodos is immediately attracted by a tiny cupboard in the center. Inside the cupboard, a small female form greets him. The tiny fairy becomes human in size when she jumps down on to the floor. She tells Anodos that he will find his way into Fairy Land the next day. Then, the fairy invites him to look into her eyes. As he does so, he is filled with an intense longing. Anodos somehow remembers his mother who died when he was a baby. As he looks deeper into the fairy's face, her eyes become like seas. Anodos finds himself standing at the window of his father's old dark study, gazing at a heaven filled with stars and the sea below. Then, he realizes the moon is shining, not on the sea, but on a bog. He says to himself, "Surely there is such a sea somewhere." Anodos hears a voice behind him say, "In Fairy Land." However, when he turns to look, the fairy has disappeared.

Chapter II—Anodos' Bedroom Transformed
Anodos awakes the next morning to discover that his washbasin has overflowed with water, now forming a stream alongside his bed. Out of the border of the carpet, also beside the bed, there is growing tall grass and daisies blown by a breeze. The carved foliage on Anodos' dressing table is also going through a metamorphosis, changing into real ivy. Above his head, the design on the bed-curtains is becoming branches and leaves, also waving in the wind. Anodos quickly gets up and dresses. Then he notices a footpath beside the stream. He follows it into a forest.

Chapter III—The Cottage of Mother & Daughter

In the forest, Anodos meets a country maiden. The girl tells Anodos to trust the Oak, Elm, and the great Beech, but to beware the changeableness of the Birch, and to shun the Ash and the Alder. The maiden departs and Anodos continues deeper into the forest where he finds a wide-open glade that is sunk in utter stillness. One wonders if MacDonald's description of the quiet glade later influenced Lewis' depiction of The Wood Between the Worlds in *The Magician's Nephew*.

Anodos continues walking on through the forest and grows hungry as noontime approaches. Eventually, he comes to a cottage where he meets the mother of the maiden. She is preparing vegetables for dinner and invites Anodos into the cottage to eat, in order to escape the gaze of the Ash. Once inside, the woman tells Anodos that he has fairy blood in him. The daughter returns home and takes up various household duties while Anodos reads from a large book containing tales of King Arthur and the Knights of the Round Table. While he is reading, the shadow of the Ash tree, in the form of a hand, falls across the blind on the cottage window. When Anodos asks the woman how they are safe from the Ash inside the cottage, she tells him that the oaks, forming the four corners of the cottage will protect them. The woman goes on to explain to Anodos about various fairies and their relation to the flora and fauna of Fairy Land. When the daughter spies outside that the Ash has departed, they conclude that it is safe for Anodos to continue on his journey. Outside the cottage Anodos and the mother and daughter meet a carnival of fairy activity in the garden. Anodos' attention is particularly drawn to a group of fairies, singing a song as they gather around a last dying primrose.

Chapter IV—Encounter with the Beech

Anodos departs from the cottage into the forest. As he is going along, the flower fairies mock him saying, "Look at him! Look at him! He has begun a story without a beginning, and it will never have any end. He! he! he! Look at him!"

Perhaps this is MacDonald's own admission that his story *is* rather dreamlike, with no beginning and no end, just a stream of consciousness. On the other hand, this may also be a confession of MacDonald's fear that having gotten this far with the story, he doesn't know where to take it from here. I suspect that Lewis and MacDonald shared a love of creating other worlds for their own sake. Thus, plot was secondary. Lewis once said,

> The starting point of the second novel, *Perelandra*, was my mental picture of the floating islands. The whole of the rest of my labours in a sense consisted of building up a world in which floating islands could exist. And then of course the story about an averted fall developed. This

is because, as you know, having got your people to this exciting country, something must happen.¹¹⁴

As Anodos progresses through the nighttime forest, the shadow of the hand of the Ash tree eventually falls upon him, sending him scurrying away in fright, as thunder crashes and torrents of rain fall from the heavens. In his headlong flight, Anodos falls at the roots of a Beech tree. The female spirit of the Beech surrounds him with her protecting arms, telling him he no longer need be afraid of the Ash. The Beech woman explains to Anodos that the Ash tree wants to bury him at his own roots in order to fill up a hole in his heart. The Beech invites Anodos to cut off some of her hair and wrap it around himself in order to ward off the Ash. Anodos does so and then falls asleep. When he awakes, he finds himself lying beneath a beech tree but the spirit of the beech is gone. As Anodos leaves that place he seems to hear the spirit of the beech whispering once more her love for him: "I may love him. I may love him; for he is a man, and I am only a beech-tree."

Chapter V—The White Lady in the Stone

As Anodos continues on his way through the forest, he eats some of its nuts and fruits for the first time. Eating the produce of Fairy Land enables him to understand what the animals are saying to one another. Anodos discovers a cave and delights to rest in its shade as he drinks from a spring of refreshing water therein. After lying in an hour-long reverie, Anodos notices a bas-relief on the wall of the cave depicting the story of Pygmalion, all about a sculptor who falls in love with a statue that he carves. The sight of this bas-relief leads Anodos to wonder if something like the story of Pygmalion actually took place in the cave. He removes the moss from the rock on which he is resting to discover that it is beautiful, white alabaster. Enclosed in the translucent rock is the form of a woman. Anodos kneels and kisses the rock, hoping thereby to awaken and release the lovely girl entombed there. This attempt fails to rouse the sleeping beauty; therefore, Anodos sings to her a song of his own instantaneous composition, inspired by the drinking of the spring-water which functions as an elixir of life. Eventually, as Anodos sings on, a white form emerges from the stone and sails away into the forest. Anodos follows the white ghost with keen anticipation.

Chapter VI—A Meeting with the Alder

Anodos is delayed in his pursuit of the white apparition by the appearance of a red knight on horseback, riding towards him, as it were, on the rays of the setting sun. Anodos remembers the story he was reading in the cottage about Sir Percival in his rusty armor. The knight warns Anodos about the beguiling beauty of the maiden of the alder tree for whom he put off his armor, thus resulting in its rusty appearance. Before Anodos can question the knight about his story, the knight rides away.

Anodos continues on, in search of the wraith that emerged from the alabaster stone. He sings to her once more a poem of his own composition in hopes that this will call the beautiful maiden back to him. No sooner has he finished singing then Anodos hears a laugh beside him and sees his white lady seated beside a thicket. She invites Anodos to her grotto and he follows her there. Once inside the cave the lady tells Anodos a strange tale that serves to fix his attention completely upon her great beauty. Anodos falls asleep and awakens to find the white maiden gone. In her stead, he meets a coffin-like human figure bearing her face. Her fingers are ripping asunder long silky tresses of hair—the very hair the spirit of the birch tree gave to protect Anodos. His white maiden turns out to be none other than the spirit of the Alder tree the knight had warned him about. The Alder then surrenders Anodos to the clutches of the Ash. However, before the Ash is able to grab hold of him, he hears the sound of axe blows. The Ash and the Alder retreat in haste, leaving Anodos to weep over his own foolishness.

Chapter VII—A Visit to a Farmhouse
Anodos leaves the cave behind and wanders aimlessly, perplexed by the question: How can beauty and ugliness dwell so close together in the same person as they did in the Alder? On the outskirts of the forest, Anodos arrives at a farmhouse. The matron of the farm feeds Anodos and discusses with him his adventures in the forest. Anodos asks this motherly figure how the spirit of the alder tree could be so beautiful when she had no heart for beauty to reside in. She explains that the Alder's desire to bewitch men and gain their love makes her more beautiful than she really is. Furthermore, she tells Anodos that he must have mistaken the spirit of the alder for his beloved white lady of the alabaster stone. She warns Anodos not to tell her husband of his adventures because her husband does not believe, as she does, in the spirits of the trees and the other goings-on in the wood. In fact, the very presence of the farmer when he arrives home makes it difficult for Anodos to believe in Fairy Land anymore until he spies the farmer's daughter sitting in the chimney-corner of the farmhouse reading a book. The daughter reminds her father that the mother is descended from a princess who was turned into a white cat by a wicked fairy. Brushing this story aside, the farmer sits down to dinner with Anodos and his family, including a son even more cynical than he is. After dinner, Anodos spends a restful night in their house. Before breakfast the next morning, the farmer's daughter informs Anodos privately that a white lady has been flitting about the house all night. After breakfast, the mother and her daughter show Anodos into the daughter's bedroom that contains a

window facing the forest. Looking out the window, Anodos sees Fairy Land again and longs to enter it. (Anodos' longing for Fairy Land parallels John's longing for the Island in Lewis' *The Pilgrim's Regress*.) Anodos is led into the forest by the farmer's son who guides him to a path that will lead him safely beyond the ogre's house, the one the farmer has warned him about (despite the farmer's lack of belief in ogres!).

Chapter VIII—The House of the Ogre

Returning deep into the forest, Anodos discovers a hut in a clearing. Inside the hut is a woman, reading by lamplight. As Anodos enters, the woman reads aloud from the ancient book in her hands: "So, then, as darkness had no beginning, neither will it ever have an end...."

Anodos gives in to an irresistible urge to open a door at the end of the hut beyond the woman, but she warns him against doing so. This warning only increases Anodos' desire and so he opens the door. At first, it appears to be a common closet, but on closer examination, Anodos finds a glimmering luminosity at the other end of the closet. He soon discovers this light to be that of the night sky at the end of a dark hallway. (Is there a parallel here to Lucy finding Narnia through the wardrobe door?) A dark human figure approaches Anodos from the other end of the hallway and passes by him into the hut. The woman explains to Anodos that the dark figure is his shadow that has found him. Suddenly, as the old woman leers at him with long, white teeth, Anodos realizes he is in the house of the ogre. He immediately departs, accompanied now by his very black shadow.

Chapter IX—Travels with the Shadow

The narrator warns us at the beginning of this chapter that he can provide no consecutive account of his wanderings from this point until he reaches the Fairy Palace. This should come as no surprise, given the dreamlike, stream-of-consciousness quality of the whole story up to this point.

This chapter deals largely with the effects of the Shadow on Anodos' journey. When he lies down in the grass for a rest and then rises, Anodos notices that the flowers and the grass where he has lain soon spring back to life; not so the flowers and the grass where the Shadow has lain; they lie dead, hopeless of resurrection.

There are other special powers displayed by Anodos' shadow. On one occasion, the shadow moves in front of Anodos and shoots out rays that wither everything around. At another stop on the journey, a fairy greets Anodos and shows him special instruments used by the fairy-gifted poet. However, when the shadow falls upon the fairy he is turned into a normal boy and his instruments are revealed as a multiplying glass[115] and a kaleidoscope.

Soon after this, Anodos meets again the rusty knight. However, the knight's armor is in better shape than when last they met. In fact, the knight has faced the Alder-tree in battle and "plunged into the torrent of mighty deeds" thus nearly washing his stain away. Anodos and the knight travel together for two days, but then the shadow comes out from behind Anodos and encompasses the knight. The two part the next day.

The worst thing to befall Anodos during this part of his journey is that he begins to be proud of his shadow, for he begins to think that the shadow is showing him the world around as it really is. Thus, Anodos is proud of not having to play the fool. However, he is soon disabused of this idea.

One bright noon a maiden carrying in her hand a globe as clear as crystal meets Anodos. He asks if he may touch the globe and the maiden gives him permission so long as he does it gently. When he touches the globe Anodos feels a gentle vibration and hears a faint, sweet sound. He touches it twice more and each time the beautiful music increases in volume.

The maiden departs at twilight and rejoins Anodos at noon, for two days running. On the third day of their journey together, the shadow enwraps the maiden but is unable to change her. Anodos is seized by an intense desire to touch the globe again. As he does so with both hands, the globe emits a harmony of sound as before. Refusing to let go, despite the maiden's entreaties, prayers and tears, the globe begins to throb in Anodos' hands until it bursts, sending up black smoke. The maiden flees, crying: "You have broken my globe!" Anodos pursues her, but loses the maiden in a tempest that suddenly breaks through the forest.

The final event of this chapter takes place when Anodos approaches a village. As Anodos gets closer to each of the inhabitants of the village, their appearance grows hideous, like the appearance of one's own image seen in a fun-house mirror. Anodos is uncertain as to the cause of this, whether it is produced by his shadow or something else.

Chapter X—Journey to the Fairy Palace

After spending a week in the village, Anodos travels through the land of the goblin-fairies, a desert region of dry sand and glittering rocks. The goblins, thankfully, leave Anodos alone because of the presence of his shadow. After travelling through this land for some time, Anodos arrives at a spring where he drinks deep of the refreshing waters. He decides, after drinking from the spring, to follow the path of the stream that feeds it. The stream eventually becomes a broad river and beside it, Anodos sits down under the shade of a horse chestnut tree and weeps tears of joy for the beauty of fairy land all around him.

Anodos continues to follow the path of the river until he comes to a small boat. He lies down inside of it and allows the boat to carry him wherever the current flows. As Anodos contemplates the reflection of the moonlight upon the river, he wonders: "Why are all reflections lovelier than what we call the reality?" He concludes: "All mirrors are magic mirrors."

In time, the river carries Anodos to a view of a "palace glimmering ghostly in the moonshine". Leaving his boat behind, Anodos ascends the hill to the palace and goes exploring within. In the palace, he discovers a door of ebony with silver lettering, glowing with phosphorescence. The letters spell out: "The Chamber of Sir Anodos". Opening the door, Anodos discovers a room that is the perfect copy of his own bedroom back home. There is a glowing fire on the hearth and a bright lamp upon a table. Anodos sits down to feast upon the plentiful meal laid out for him on the table, and he is waited upon by invisible hands.[116] After dinner, Anodos sits by the fire for a while and then takes himself to bed where he hopes to sleep peacefully and truly waken in his own room to discover that Fairy Land has been only a vision of the night.

Chapter XI—Exploring the Fairy Palace

Anodos awakes to find he is still in the Fairy Palace and has been provided with a suit of fresh clothing perfectly adapted to his tastes. Anodos goes out exploring around the palace; however, he finds, due to the white marble all around, that the palace is too dazzling in the blazing sun for his mortal eyes to take in. He doesn't even bother to think about his shadow until he lies down in the grass in the grounds of the palace and looks to see if the shadow is still there. The shadow is faintly discernible, which Anodos finds most discouraging. Still, he hopes to find within the environs of the Fairy Palace a shadow of light to dispel the shadow of darkness.

The heat of the day causes Anodos to retreat and conduct further exploration within the palace. There he finds a beautiful room with a large pool. He takes off his clothes and dives in. Beneath the surface of the water, Anodos sees a vast ocean, but when he surfaces, he finds himself once again in the same room inside the palace. After swimming for a bit, Anodos removes himself from the pool and dresses. As he walks about the palace, he finds that he can now see, but faintly, the fairy inhabitants thereof. Anodos spends many days in the palace, fed and attended by the fairies, bathing each day in the fairy pool, untroubled by his shadow that he assumes is lurking somewhere.

On his third day living in the Fairy Palace, Anodos discovers the library. The books in this library differ from those in our world, in that while Anodos reads from them, the truths or the stories contained therein truly come alive; consequently, Anodos would forget, for a time, that he was reading at all. Rather, he became the chief character in the story or history that he was reading; then he would awake to suddenly find it all a dream.

Chapter XII—The Story within the Story

Anodos, as narrator, begins this chapter by explaining that the stars have more power over human destiny than is normally supposed. There is a delicate interconnection between every created thing in the universe. He then goes on to explain that children are not born in Fairy Land as they are in our world. Rather, in certain seasons of the year, especially in summer, the female fairies go looking for children and find them, often beside a riverbank, just as children in our world go looking for and picking wildflowers.

The narrator goes on to explain that male and female fairies differ in that the men alone have arms, whereas the women have wings. Furthermore, these wings are of different colors depending upon the season in which they were born.

One evening in the summer, Anodos stands with a group of male and female fairies on a rock overhanging the sea. Asked about how children are born in our world, Anodos makes a vague reply. Once the truth of his explanation dawns on some of the female fairies they stalk away in some disgust, one even to her death.

At this point, the reader discovers that what he has been treated to in this chapter is merely what Anodos has been reading in a book in the library, but while Anodos reads, it seems alive and real to him, as it has to the reader of *Phantastes*. Anodos as narrator closes this chapter by retelling a story from the book he is reading about a fairy maiden, born at the close of autumn, who sets out to find springtime. In the end, she lies down on the border between winter and spring and dies. However, Anodos believes that in this very place a new fairy child is born to take her place.

Chapter XIII—The Story of Cosmo

This chapter marks the halfway point through *Phantastes* and it is the longest chapter in the book. In this chapter, Anodos tries to reproduce one of the stories from one of the fairy books in the library of the fairy palace.

The story is that of Cosmo von Wehrstahl, a student at the University of Prague. Cosmo discovers in a musty shop one day a mirror with elaborate carving on its frame. He greatly desires to purchase the mirror, which, despite its age, offers a very clear reflection. However, the price is too dear. The shopkeeper offers the mirror to Cosmo at a quarter of the price because he knew Cosmo's dead father. Cosmo purchases the mirror despite its cost still being very great. The shopkeeper parts with the mirror on the condition that if Cosmo ever wishes to get rid of it he will let the shopkeeper have the first offer.

Cosmo takes his purchase back to his room at the top of a tall tower. He hangs the mirror on the wall and as he gazes into it, he realizes that the mirror reflects a room very much like his own, yet different. The main difference is that as he gazes into the mirror he sees a female form, all in white, glide into the room and lie upon the couch. When Cosmo turns and looks at the "real" couch in the room, the lady is not there, but when he turns back to the mirror she is.

Noticing that the lady in white responds to various things in his room, Cosmo sets about removing things she dislikes, such as a skeleton, and furnishing the room in a fashion to please her. The lady continues to appear to Cosmo every evening until one night she does not come.

Cosmo is desolate. He determines that he is going to bring the lady to himself, out of the mirror, by magic. He collects the necessary materials, performs the conjuration, and after several attempts the lady leaves her room in the mirror and enters Cosmo's own.

The lady urges him, "Cosmo, if thou lovest me, set me free, even from thyself: break the mirror." Taking the chance that he may not see the lady again, Cosmo takes his sword to break the mirror, but before he can do so a terrible clap of thunder seems to break in the room itself. Cosmo is knocked unconscious and when he awakes, the mirror and the lady are both gone. He is seized with a brain fever and takes to his bed for weeks.

Once he recovers his reason and strength, Cosmo goes in search of the mirror. The shopkeeper, from whom he bought the mirror, says he knows nothing of its whereabouts. At a party, Cosmo hears the story of Princess von Hohenweiss who has recently taken ill at the loss of an antique mirror that used to stand in her dressing room.

Cosmo goes in search of a man named Von Steinwald, whom he thinks may be in possession of the mirror. Meanwhile, the lady is set free of her enchantment and goes in search of Cosmo. They meet on a bridge in the city, and Cosmo dies in her arms, mortally wounded, apparently from a duel with Von Steinwald.

Chapter XIV—Halls of Statues

Returning to Anodos in the Fairy Palace, we find him discovering a room with crimson curtains and a red throne-like chair. Anodos sits in the chair for hours on end seeing various visions in his mind's eye. He returns to the hall and the chair every morning, sometimes sitting in the chair and dreaming away, or walking about and enacting whole dramas in his mind, or singing a song he feels it urgent to sing due to some unseen muse in the palace. Sometimes the music in his soul is so intense he thinks there must be people dancing somewhere. On one evening, when this same thought seizes him, Anodos decides to lift up one of the crimson curtains. Behind the curtain, he finds another hall filled with statues, illuminated by a great, crimson, globe-shaped light. Around the lamp, there shines this message: Touch not!¹¹⁷

The next time Anodos explores the hall of statues he decides to venture further. He finds behind yet another crimson curtain another hall also filled with statutes. Yet these are unlike the first, for in the first hall Anodos had the sense that the statues had just finished dancing and returned to their pedestals the moment before he entered the room. Anodos continues his exploration on another night and finds twelve such halls filled with statues both ancient and modern.

Anodos dreams, one night, of entering one of the halls to actually find the statues alive and dancing. He also finds, in his dream, the lady who came out of the white marble in the cave. However, Anodos' shadow descends and hides the lady from him.

The next evening, Anodos goes in search of the hall and the statues in his dream, hoping to find the lady from the white marble. In the tenth hall, he finds a pedestal, identical to the one in his dream where the lady stood, except that it is empty. After numerous attempts, Anodos is able to enter one of the halls and actually catch the statues in the act of dancing. However, when he reaches the tenth hall, the pedestal, where he hopes to find the lady of the white marble, is empty, except for the faint glimmer of white feet resting on the black pedestal.

Chapter XV—Singing into Visibility

Anodos tries to come up with a song to sing that will cause the lady of the white marble to be revealed. When he unleashes his song, the dancers in the hall return to their pedestals where they resume their statue-like nature. Anodos takes a harp from the hand of one of the statues. As Anodos plays the harp and sings, the lady of the white marble is slowly revealed upon her pedestal, starting from the feet upward.

Chapter XVI—In Pursuit of the White Lady

Once the white lady is fully visible Anodos follows his irresistible urge to wrap his arms around the statue. As he does so, and removes her from the pedestal, she becomes a living being. However, the lady runs away crying: "You should not have touched me!"

Anodos follows her but comes to a roadblock, a door with silver lettering conveying this message: "No one enters here without the leave of the Queen." Anodos ignores the warning and opens the door. On the other side, he finds himself standing on a windy hillside filled with tombstones. The Fairy Palace is nowhere to be seen. A white figure sails past Anodos crying: "You should have sung to me!" She disappears behind a tombstone, but when Anodos looks there, he sees nothing but a large hole. Waiting for daylight, he sits down and weeps.

Chapter XVII—Into the Abyss

By daylight, Anodos detects a natural spiral staircase descending along the edge of the abyss and decides to follow this path in search of his lady in white. When he goes as far as the stairs will take him, he makes his way into an underground tunnel.

Along the way, Anodos meets goblins. They gather in a circle and sing the same song to Anodos that he sang to make the white lady visible. The goblins tell Anodos that he won't be able to have the white lady because she is saving herself for a better man. Anodos accepts this news with great humility and so the goblins let him go.

As Anodos continues on his way singing, he eventually meets an elderly woman. This commonplace looking woman taunts Anodos about how nice it would be to walk with a pretty girl by his side, even in this underground world. Anodos replies: it depends on who the girl is. At this, the woman's appearance is transformed into that of a true beauty and a lovely landscape appears all around them. The woman pleads for Anodos to stay with her but he draws back. Anodos hears an infernal laugh and the beautiful girl changes back into an ugly woman again. She promises Anodos that he will see his white lady. However, Anodos tells her that his seeing his white lady does not depend upon her. With that, Anodos turns and continues on his way.

Chapter XVIII—Into the Sea

As Anodos continues on his journey, the tunnel grows smaller until he has to crawl on his hands and knees. However, he perseveres, both in hope of seeing his white lady, but also in hope of leaving Fairy Land, of which he is now quite weary.

Eventually the tunnel leads Anodos back to the daylight where he stands before a wintry sea. Having nowhere else to go but forward Anodos walks along a promontory out into the raging sea, the waves threatening to knock him over at each step. At the end of the promontory, he dives headfirst into the waters and swims ever deeper.

When he comes again to the surface he eventually meets a little boat and climbs aboard. After resting in the bottom of the boat for some time, Anodos eventually sits up and looks around him to find that he is no longer sailing a storm-tossed, wintry sea, but rather a calm ocean in the midst of a perpetual, summer twilight.

When Anodos looks down into the waters, he sees a great wonder beneath the waves, a vision of his entire Past. Anodos falls asleep in the boat where he experiences the most comforting dreams. When he awakes, he finds the boat floating beside the grassy shore of a little island.

Chapter XIX—On the Island

On the island, Anodos finds a cottage. In the cottage, Anodos discovers an old woman—older and more beautiful than any he has yet met in Fairy Land. The old woman feeds Anodos and he finds the cottage to be a great place of refuge and repose. The woman sings to him some old ballads set to ancient tunes. One of them is about a knight, Sir Aglovaile,[118] who seeks a ghost-like maiden in white. However, when he embraces her she turns into a corpse and then the ghost never visits him again.

Anodos falls asleep while the old woman sings on; then he wakes to find her by the front door weeping. She turns and faces another door, there is one in the center of each of the four walls of the cottage, and when she faces this door, rather than weeping, she sighs. When she turns to the third door, a cry as of fear or pain escapes her lips, and when she turns to the fourth door she shudders and stands as still as a statue. However, after she looks upward a beautiful smile crosses her face and she continues with her work, tending the fire in the fireplace and spinning at her wheel.

Anodos desires to explore the island but the old woman bids him stay. She warns him that he will not see what he expects to see on the island and that whenever he wants to return to the cottage he must look for a special red mark which she reveals to him.

The whole scene changes when Anodos steps out of the cottage. The cottage itself becomes the barn on his father's farm and he sees his brothers running through the field. He joins them and when he goes to sleep that night in the same bed with his favorite brother, their last words to one another are not ones of kindness, due to an argument between them, despite the delights of the day spent together. In the morning, Anodos' favorite brother goes for a swim in the river and drowns. Anodos departs his father's cottage, weeping over this news and when he arrives at the barn, he sees the special red mark the old woman told him about. When he opens the door of the barn, it becomes the cottage on the island again with the old woman inside sitting at her spinning wheel.

After being encouraged by another song from the old woman, Anodos opens the door of sighs and finds himself in a lordly hall. Beside a blazing fire on the hearth sits a lady waiting for someone. She resembles Anodos' lady in white but she obviously isn't waiting for Anodos. Soon, the knight of the soiled armor enters and the lady welcomes him with great affection. His armor now shines brightly and as he sits by the hearth, eating and drinking what his lady provides for him, they talk together about Anodos. The lady's love for her knight is obviously greater than her love for Anodos, though she is grateful to him for freeing her from the marble by her song. The lady and the knight depart into another room. However, when Anodos tries to follow them through the same door he finds himself back in the cottage with the old woman.

Again, the old woman sings to Anodos and once again, he is encouraged in his love for the white lady whom he loves more than ever. He gets up and goes through the door of Dismay, finding himself on the other side of the door in a crowded street. He sees a girl he once loved when he was a teenager. Not wanting to face her, he turns away and goes to see the room where she lived and where they used to spend time together. However, when Anodos goes into the room he finds himself in a church instead, where he sees his former beloved walking, dressed in white. Is she a ghost? Soon, Anodos realizes he is among the tombs of his ancestors. He asks that a dead woman should comfort him. A kiss alights on his lips and a hand grasps his. Anodos then stumbles into one of the stones covering the entrance to a vault, but when he pushes on it he finds himself in the cottage with the old woman and she sings to him once more.[119]

After the old woman sings to him, Anodos falls into a deep, peaceful sleep. When he awakes he finds the old woman blocking the way to the fourth door, but he rushes past her and through the final portal, as the woman cries after him, "Don't go there my child!" However, Anodos remembers nothing more after that. He awakes to find his head in the lap of the old woman who smiles at him through her tears. The woman explains that she had to go through the fourth door to rescue Anodos, and because she has done so, the waters are rising around her cottage. Therefore, she tells Anodos he must leave. She begs him to remember that whatever sorrow he endures in life that she knows something about it that would make it more sweet than bitter. The old woman explains that they are not on an island. She takes Anodos through the third door and shows him where to follow the isthmus to escape the rising waters. As the old woman embraces Anodos he feels like he is leaving his mother for the first time. She urges him to go and "do something worth doing".

Chapter XX—In the Tower

Anodos gets safely across the isthmus, and after walking for some time he comes upon a tower where he hears, coming from inside, the clang of metal against an anvil. When the sound ceases for a moment, Anodos knocks on the door to the tower. A bare-chested young man welcomes Anodos; he bears a sword still glowing from the furnace. Inside the tower, beside the hearth, Anodos meets another young man who, like the first, is half undressed. The two young men are brothers. The elder of the two, who welcomed Anodos at the door, addresses him as "Brother" and invites Anodos to rest until they finish their work. Anodos asks why they address him as brother and thus the elder of the two young men proceeds to tell him a story.

The elder brother explains that their father is the king of this country and that before they were born three giant brothers appeared in the land and restored an old, broken-down castle. At first, the giants were peaceful. However, in time they began to steal provisions from some of the neighboring country houses. The father of the two young men sought to capture the castle but his men were killed in the attempt. The giants then began to take hostage some of their neighbors. Many tried to defeat the giants, all to no avail. The two brothers, also wanting to defeat the giants, sought the wisdom of an old woman. She instructed the brothers to exercise their bodies long and hard for the fight and to prepare their armor. She also promised she would send a third brother, Anodos, to help them in their struggle.

Anodos decides to join the two brothers in their fight against the three giants. While they continue forging their armor together, Anodos sings songs of his own composition to strengthen and encourage them in their task.

Chapter XXI—The Battle with the Giants

Anodos and the two brothers are surprised at their tower by the approach of the three giants. With no time to put on their armor, each of the three "brothers" pick up their favorite weapons and go out to face their foes. By some miracle, all three giants are killed in the conflict, but Anodos is the only one of the three "brothers" to survive. After the battle, Anodos suddenly looks behind himself and sees his Shadow lying black on the ground.

Anodos announces the victory to the neighbors all around. They set upon the giants' castle and release the prisoners there. Then Anodos determines to take the bodies of the two brothers to their father.

The father-king, upon hearing Anodos' tale, dubs him a knight. Anodos spends no little time at the king's palace, enjoying the company of his courtiers. However, the entire time Anodos is troubled by the thought of his Shadow still lingering somewhere nearby. Thus, he determines to leave and find the lady whom the elder prince had loved and tell her of his death.

Chapter XXII—Trapped in another Tower

On the third day of his journey, Anodos meets a youth on the edge of a forest that warns him about possible enchantments therein. Anodos enters the forest nonetheless and immediately feels relieved of the presence of his constant companion, the Shadow. As Anodos begins to reflect on his past, and especially on his battle with the giants, he is filled with pride at the thought of his accomplishments and considers himself a knight worthy to be compared with Sir Galahad.

Anodos then meets a resplendent knight of mighty size who wears armor and rides a horse exactly like Anodos' own. Anodos seeks to pass the knight, but his courage fails him and he is unable. The knight bids Anodos to follow him and he does. Eventually they arrive at a square tower in the midst of the forest where the knight locks Anodos in, alone, along with his Shadow.

Anodos sits down, disconsolate within the tower. However, that night when the moon shines through an opening in the roof of the tower and onto Anodos' head, everything around him is transformed. The walls vanish and he finds himself sitting beneath a beech tree on the edge of a forest in open country. However, when the sun rises, Anodos is back in the locked tower again with his black shadow beside him. Every night, the same pattern repeats itself, until the moon is no longer able to reach Anodos in his lonely tower.

One night, Anodos dreams of his home and longs to be free. About noon, on the next day, Anodos hears the singing of a woman. In response to the woman's song, Anodos tries the door of the tower and finds he is able to open it. Going outside he finds a young woman by a tree blocking the door. It is the same woman whose globe Anodos broke. The young woman explains that she took the fragments of her globe to the Fairy Queen. Rather than give her back her globe in mended condition, the Queen sent the young woman away with a better gift—the ability to sing. Wherever she goes her song delivers people, and now it has delivered Anodos from his imprisonment in the tower.

Anodos begs the young woman's forgiveness for breaking her globe. She tells Anodos there is nothing to forgive. Instead, she thanks him and bids him farewell. Anodos, too, departs after stripping off his armor and laying it at the root of the beech tree. For the first time he knows the delight of being lowly, and he realizes that his shadow is gone.

At the end of this chapter, MacDonald writes, "Self will come to life even in the slaying of self; but there is ever something deeper and stronger than it, which will emerge at last from the unknown abysses of the soul…"[120] In reading these lines I was reminded of the undragoning of Eustace in *The Voyage of the Dawn Treader*. Lewis and MacDonald both emphasize this point, that every human being has many selves to slay, many layers of dragon skin that have to be removed.

Chapter XXIII—Travels with the Knight

Before Anodos has travelled very far he hears another voice—the voice of another knight singing as he rides along on a strange beast. As the knight draws near, Anodos realizes that the strange beast is actually a dead dragon that the knight carries on the back of his horse. The knight turns out to be the one whom Anodos met earlier, with the soiled armor. Anodos offers his services to the knight as his squire.

Soon they come upon a cottage, out of which darts a woman crying out to the knight, asking if he has found her daughter. The knight tells the woman that he has found her daughter, but that she is wounded and he has left her with the hermit. The knight lays the dragon at the cottage door and the man of the house thanks him, while the woman rushes off to find her daughter. The knight urges the man to bury the dragon.

Knight and squire take their rest in the cottage. As Anodos observes his master, he decides that his white lady was right to prefer the knight to himself. When the mother returns with her terribly wounded daughter, the knight tenderly binds her wounds. Then, after a meal and instruction on how to treat the child's wounds, knight and squire depart.

As the knight and Anodos travel on together, they take turns riding the horse, and the knight tells Anodos the story of the young maiden whom he rescued. Eventually they arrive at a sanctuary enclosed by yew trees. Inside they find men in white robes, standing silent with swords at their sides. As night falls, and the stars shine down upon them through the open roof of the enclosure, a young girl stands beside Anodos, clothed in a similar fashion to the male priests. Suddenly, a star as big as the sun shines down upon them and a great song arises from the men in white. At the far end of the enclosure stands a throne on a platform. The priests ascend to the throne on which sits a majestic looking figure. After bowing before the throne, the priests force a young man among them to enter through a door in the pedestal to the throne. Next, a girl is subjected to a similar fate. What happens to each victim, Anodos never learns, but he is convinced that the entire proceeding is evil; whereas the knight does not seem to be aware of anything wrong going on.

Anodos borrows the white garment worn by the girl standing next to him so that he will look like the others in the room. Thus clad, Anodos mounts the throne and removes the wooden image he finds there. Beneath the image there is a hole out of which a wolf bounds, causing Anodos to tumble down the steps from the throne. Anodos tries to kill the beast with his bare hands as all the white-clad priests come rushing on, swords drawn, but then Anodos faints and knows no more.

Chapter XXIV—In the Land of Death

Anodos lies dead in his coffin, but is able to observe the knight and his lady weeping over his body. The knight explains to his lady how Anodos killed the wolf but died in the process and how he was able to bring back the dead body of his squire for burial. The lady remarks that Anodos has died well.

Though Anodos' body lies dead in the coffin, his spirit rejoices in its repose, breathing "the clear mountain-air of the land of Death." (This part of the story is reminiscent of the clear air on Aslan's mountain in *The Silver Chair*.) Even when the coffin is buried, Anodos feels the great heart of mother earth beating her life into his. As he hears the footsteps of his friends above the grave, he is able to rise into the face of a primrose and look upon the countenance of his beloved lady. She picks the primrose and kisses it, but then the flower withers and so Anodos must depart from it. He ascends to a cloud and meditates on the ways in which he will tend to his friends, wait upon them, and haunt them with his love.

However, Anodos then experiences a pang and a terrible shudder. Writhing, as in the throws of death, he convulses and becomes conscious once again "of a more limited, even a bodily and earthly life."

Chapter XXV—Home Again
Anodos finds himself lying in the open air, in the early morning, just before sunrise. At first, Anodos is afraid when he sees his shadow, but then he realizes it is only a natural shadow. As he looks around, he realizes he is home.

His sisters receive him with a joy mixed with awe, for on the day of his disappearance they found his room flooded and a mist hanging about the castle. His sisters tell him that he was gone for twenty-one days.

Anodos wonders whether he will be able to translate the experience of his travels into the language of everyday life. In fact, George MacDonald spent most of his life, after writing *Phantastes*, trying to translate the spiritual messages of that book into the form of the common novel. However, at least one of his readers, one Clive Staples Lewis, would always value MacDonald's fantasies far more than his "commonplace" writings.

There are at least three spiritual messages that the young Lewis would have received from a reading of *Phantastes*. One concerns the nature of passion. Through the course of the story, Anodos dies to self and thereby his passions are refined and made pure. Second, Lewis would have learned something, consciously or unconsciously, about spiritual growth. There are many passages in *Phantastes* that deal with this subject. A third theme in the book has to do with the nature and power of love. By the end of the story, Anodos discovers that he is able to love others without needing to be loved in return. He learns that love, in its essence, is self-giving.[121]

Anodos closes his narrative by saying, "Thus I, who set out to find my Ideal, came back rejoicing that I had lost my Shadow." In the same way, C. S. Lewis too would spend his early life searching for the Ideal, and in 1931, he would finally find what he was looking for and rejoice in the losing of his shadow.

G. K. Chesterton

THE EVERLASTING MAN
BY G. K. CHESTERTON

Lewis' Reading of Chesterton

When C. S. Lewis went up to Oxford for the first time in December 1916, he had never heard of the contemporary writer, G. K. Chesterton. This simple fact reveals something of Lewis' preference for "older works", a preference to which he would hold throughout his life. Lewis felt that this preference was a safeguard against "crazes" for new authors whose merits had not yet been fully tested. In fact, among "famous" authors of the time, William Butler Yeats was the only one in whom Lewis displayed any interest.[122]

Lewis' undergraduate studies at Oxford were interrupted by his involvement in the First World War. He landed in France on his nineteenth birthday—November 29, 1917. He was eventually wounded during service in the trenches and then transferred to a hospital in England where he spent the remainder of the war. However, before this, he fell ill with trench fever, and spent the month of February 1918, recuperating in a hospital at Le Treport.

It was during this first wartime convalescence that Lewis read Chesterton—a volume of his essays.[123] Lewis later said that Chesterton made an "immediate conquest" of him, but he did not know why. It does seem strange that an avowedly Christian author would appeal to Lewis during this, the darkest period of his atheism. However, Lewis enjoyed Chesterton's humor—the kind that is "the 'bloom' on dialectic itself". He also liked Chesterton for his goodness despite the fact that Lewis had no intention of pursuing goodness himself. Lewis later drew the following lesson from the experience: "In reading Chesterton, as in reading MacDonald, I did not know what I was letting myself in for. A young man who wishes to remain a sound Atheist cannot be too careful of his reading."[124]

Over the course of the next several years, a number of volumes from Chesterton's pen would find their way on to C. S. Lewis' reading list. Since he was living the life of a rather impoverished student,[125] Lewis seldom purchased the books he read for pleasure at this stage in his life. Rather, he would check out books, unrelated to his degree, from the Oxford Union library. It was in this fashion that he read Chesterton's play, *Magic*, in May 1922,[126] Chesterton's book on the poet, Robert Browning, later that same year,[127] and

Chesterton's *Life of St. Francis* in 1924.[128] Lewis by no means always agreed with Chesterton; in fact, sometimes he found him irritating. The volume on Browning he thought to be "thoroughly bad" and full of silly generalizations. Lewis thought Chesterton's scholarship rather slipshod at times. About his chapter in *Browning* on *The Ring and the Book*, Lewis felt there was nothing to show that Chesterton had actually read it.[129] Nonetheless, Lewis would later write that: "Chesterton had more sense than all the other moderns put together; bating, of course, his Christianity."[130]

Because Lewis found Chesterton to be a very intriguing author, it came natural to him to read his new works as soon as they were published. Thus, he possibly read *The Everlasting Man* not long after it hit the bookstores and the libraries in 1925 or early 1926.[131] Lewis later said that in this book Chesterton helped him to see "the whole Christian outline of history set out in a form that seemed to make sense".[132]

By this time, Lewis was ensconced as a tutor of English language and literature at Magdalen College. Having more leisure for pleasure reading he was using available moments to read even more of Chesterton, consuming four of his books from May to July of 1926: *Club of Queer Trades*,[133] *The Lunatic at Large*,[134] *Eugenics and Other Evils*,[135] and *Bernard Shaw*.[136]

However, Lewis kept going back to *The Everlasting Man*. By the spring of 1929[137], he had become a theist. He had now concluded that: "Paganism had been only the childhood of religion, or only a prophetic dream." The key question was: "Where was the thing full grown?" This is where he found *The Everlasting Man* to be especially helpful.[138] By September 1931, Lewis had his answer: Christianity.

Lewis later ranked his discovery of Chesterton on a level with his first encounter with the works of George MacDonald, William Morris, and Charles Williams.[139] He often referred to Williams' novels as "theological shockers", a genre that he believed Chesterton had invented.[140] However, Lewis always insisted that Chesterton had more of an influence on his thought, rather than his imagination per se.[141] Though he liked Chesterton's fiction and his poetry, particularly *The Ballad of the White Horse*,[142] he felt more indebted to him as a "controversialist".[143]

Lewis believed that Chesterton's most important influence on his thought was in the realm of bringing him back to Christian faith.[144] Thus, he often recommended *The Everlasting Man* to others.[145] In giving his own BBC broadcast talks on Christianity in the 1940s, Lewis felt he was only watering the wine of Chesterton's works[146] and he was glad to hear that his friend, Dom Bede Griffiths, found a "Chestertonian quality" in his autobiography, *Surprised by Joy*.[147]

Chesterton's Life

Gilbert Keith Chesterton opened his 1936 autobiography with these memorable words:

> Bowing down in blind credulity, as is my custom, before mere authority and the tradition of the elders, superstitiously swallowing a story I could not test at the time by experiment or private judgment, I am firmly of opinion that I was born on the 29th of May, 1874, on Campden Hill, Kensington; and baptized according to the formularies of the Church of England in the little church of St. George opposite the large Waterworks Tower that dominated that ridge. I do not allege any significance in the relation of the two buildings; and I indignantly deny that the church was chosen because it needed the whole waterpower of West London to turn me into a Christian.[148]

Gilbert's father, Edward Chesterton, was "the head of a hereditary business of house agents and surveyors, which had already been established for some three generations in Kensington."[149] Gilbert's mother, Marie Grosjean, came from a family of twenty-three children. Gilbert inherited his middle name from his maternal grandmother who was from an Aberdeen family of Keiths.[150] Gilbert's maternal grandfather was a Wesleyan lay preacher.[151] Perhaps Gilbert inherited his grandfather's oratorical gifts, just as C. S. Lewis may have inherited similar gifts from his great grandfather, also a Methodist minister.[152]

Around the time of his younger brother Cecil's birth, when Gilbert was five, the family moved to 11 Warwick Gardens, Kensington.[153] Gilbert is reported to have welcomed his brother's birth with the remark: "Now I shall always have an audience."[154] Years later, Chesterton said of his relationship with his brother, "we never stopped arguing; and we never once quarreled."[155] There was also a younger sister, Beatrice, who died when Gilbert was very young. He remembered her falling off a rocking horse, but did not remember her death.[156]

Unlike C. S. Lewis, G. K. Chesterton was a bit slow in his intellectual development as a child. He did not talk very much before the age of three and did not read until he was eight.[157] He more than made up for both of these deficiencies in his later life: talking, reading, and writing more than most people of his era. Like Lewis, once he did learn to read, he was a lover of fairy tales. In particular, George MacDonald's *The Princess and the Goblin* made a difference to his whole existence, helping Chesterton "to see things in a certain way from the start."[158]

Chesterton went first to Colet Court and then to St. Paul's School, founded in 1509 by John Colet, Dean of St. Paul's Cathedral. Chesterton's parents enrolled him at St. Paul's in January 1887 at the age of thirteen. The school has had a number of distinguished scholars: Milton and Pepys just to name two.[159] By attending school as a day boy, Chesterton avoided some of the horrors of boarding school life that were to have such a powerful affect on the life of C. S. Lewis. During his time at St. Paul's, Chesterton began writing and sketching in journals. He was also a self-styled member of the Junior Debating Club and contributor to *The Debater*, the informal journal of this student-formed club.[160] In his final year at St. Paul's, Gilbert entered a contest for a prize poem and won. His subject was St. Francis Xavier.[161] C. S. Lewis achieved a similar feat at a slightly younger age with his poem "Carpe Diem after Horace" in the meter of Tennyson's "Locksley Hall".[162]

Unlike Lewis, Chesterton was not a very good student. "The idea that I had come to school to work was too grotesque to cloud my mind for an instant."[163] What Chesterton did do at St. Paul's was to form a number of important, lifelong friendships. One of these was with Lucian Oldershaw, another with E. C. Bentley, both members of their own self-styled Junior Debating Club. The friendships Lewis only began to enjoy at university were a much earlier discovery for Chesterton. However, for both men male friendship was a very important component of a happy and full life.

In 1892, Gilbert's friends went off to Oxford and Cambridge while he entered the Slade School of Art; he also attended lectures in English literature at University College, London.[164] During this time, Gilbert became an extreme skeptic. He felt as if everything might be a dream. His temptations were more in the psychic rather than the physical realm. He dabbled in spiritualism, often playing with a Ouija board. Some of his friends, seeing his drawings of this period, thought Gilbert might be going mad.[165] Intriguingly, Lewis' life followed a similar pattern in that there was a period of time in which he too had an interest in the occult.[166]

Chesterton's years at The Slade were not spent in complete idleness. He was reading good literature, like that of Walt Whitman, Browning, William Morris and Richard Le Gallienne, among others.[167] Furthermore, this was the period of Chesterton's first published writing outside of *The Debater*. It all began with meeting fellow student, Ernest Hodder Williams who belonged to the family that ran the publishing house, Hodder & Stoughton. Ernest gave Gilbert some art books to review for *The Bookman*, a monthly paper published by Hodder. Chesterton later said, "I had discovered the easiest of all professions, which I have pursued ever since."[168] He also had poetry published in *The Outlook*[169] and *The Speaker*[170] as well as articles like "The Diabolist" in the *Daily News*.[171]

In the end, Chesterton left The Slade without a degree in 1895. He took up a job with Mr. Redway, a publisher of spiritualist literature. Eventually, he moved on to the publishing firm of Fisher Unwin.[172]

One year after leaving school, Chesterton met and fell in love with Frances Blogg, whom he married in 1901.[173] At first Gilbert was startled by the fact that Frances "actually practiced a religion. This was something utterly unaccountable both to me and to the whole fussy culture in which she lived."[174] Thus, Frances led Gilbert to faith in Christ. Years later he wrote to her:

> Therefore I bring these rhymes to you
> Who brought the Cross to me.[175]

Not only did Frances introduce Gilbert to real faith in Christ, as a committed Anglo-Catholic, she put Gilbert in touch with a number of clergymen and other Anglican friends.[176] Frances was not only responsible for leading Gilbert to faith, but for keeping him properly dressed and organized in his everyday life. Without her, Gilbert truly would have been lost. The story is seemingly legendary, but it is true: on one occasion, Gilbert sent Frances a telegram saying: "Am in Market Harborough. Where ought I to be?"[177]

By the time of his marriage to Frances, Gilbert had left Fisher Unwin and was earning a living by his own writing.[178] In the autumn of 1899, he began to write regularly for the *Speaker*.[179] Chesterton and some of his friends from this weekly newspaper who were against the Boer War frequented a little restaurant in Soho. It was there in 1900 that Chesterton met fellow writer, Hilaire Belloc.[180] Their friendship was to be so vital that the atheist, George Bernard Shaw, another friend and sparring partner of Chesterton, would refer to the two as Chester-Belloc. The same year that Chesterton met Belloc he also had published two volumes of poetry: *Greybeards at Play* and *The Wild Knight and Other Poems*.[181]

Poetry was obviously not the only thing that Chesterton was writing at this time. In 1901, his first book of essays was published entitled *The Defendant*. This collection of essays had already appeared in *The Speaker*. The book encountered a mixed reception. One reviewer wrote, "Paradox ought to be used like onions to season the salad. Mr. Chesterton's salad is all onions. Paradox has been defined as 'truth standing on her head to attract attention'. Mr. Chesterton makes truth cut her throat to attract attention."[182] The use of paradox became a trademark of Chesterton's writing style, so much so that C. S. Lewis would later say, "young people won't read Chesterton. I don't think they like paradox."[183]

Perhaps Chesterton's biggest break came in 1903 when he was commissioned to write the "English Men of Letters" series which would eventually include biographies on Robert Browning, Thomas Carlyle, Leo

Tolstoy, Thackeray, and Tennyson. Stephen Gwynn described the experience from the publisher's side:

> On my advice the Macmillans had asked him [Chesterton] to do Browning in the "English Men of Letters," when he was still not quite arrived. Old Mr. Craik, the Senior Partner, sent for me and I found him in white fury, with Chesterton's proofs corrected in pencil; or rather not corrected; there were still thirteen errors uncorrected on one page; mostly in quotations from Browning. A selection from a Scotch ballad had been quoted from memory and three of the four lines were wrong. I wrote to Chesterton saying that the firm thought the book was going to "disgrace" them. His reply was like the trumpeting of a crushed elephant. But the book was a huge success.[184]

That same year, 1903, Chesterton began debating Robert Blatchford in the pages of *The Clarion*.[185] In this debate, Chesterton adopted a position on the relation of Christianity to pagan myth that Lewis himself would adopt many years later.

> Mr. Blatchford and his school point out that there are many myths parallel to the Christian story; that there were Pagan Christs, and Red Indian Incarnations, and Patagonian Crucifixions, for all I know or care. But does not Mr. Blatchford see the other side of the fact? If the Christian God really made the human race, would not the human race tend to rumours and perversions of the Christian God? If the centre of our life is a certain fact, would not people far from the centre have a muddled version of that fact? If we are so made that a Son of God must deliver us, is it odd that Patagonians should dream of a Son of God?[186]

In 1904, the debate with Blatchford continued and other significant developments were brewing in Chesterton's life. His book on *Browning* was gaining him great attention in literary circles. Thus, Sir Oliver Lodge asked Chesterton to become a candidate for the Chair of Literature at Birmingham University. However, Gilbert had no desire to be a professor and thus declined the honor.[187] Gilbert was never as good a lecturer as he was a writer, and he knew it. His voice was not very strong, and when speaking in front of a microphone he was known to hold his notes between his mouth and the mic. One observer wrote this:

> I remember the manner of his lecture. It seemed to be written on a hundred pieces of variously shaped paper, written in ink and pencil (of all colours) and in chalk. All the pages were in a splendid and startling disorder and I remember being at first a little disappointed. Then the papers were abandoned and G.K.C. talked.[188]

Instead of accepting the Chair at Birmingham, Chesterton continued what he was best at—writing. He published his first novel in 1904, entitled *The Napoleon of Notting Hill*, the story of a war between the London suburbs, a story that grew out of Chesterton's meditations on the Boer War. He considered this his first important book. He once told how the book came about in this way:

> I was "broke"—only ten shillings in my pocket. Leaving my worried wife, I went down Fleet Street, got a shave, and then ordered for myself, at the Cheshire Cheese, an enormous luncheon of my favourite dishes and a bottle of wine. It took my all, but I could then go to my publishers fortified. I told them I wanted to write a book and outlined the story of "Napoleon of Notting Hill." But I must have twenty pounds, I said, before I begin.
>
> "We will send it to you on Monday."
>
> "If you want the book," I replied, "you will have to give it to me today as I am disappearing to write it." They gave it.[189]

Before the end of 1904, Chesterton met John O'Connor, the man who would serve as the model for his fictional character Father Brown. The two men became friends when they met at the house of a mutual friend in Keighley, Yorkshire, and walked over the moors together. "On their second meeting Father O'Connor had startled, indeed almost shattered Gilbert, with certain rather lurid knowledge of human depravity which he had acquired in the course of his priestly experience." Thus, the idea of writing a story about "a priest with a knowledge of evil deeper than that of the criminal he is converting" was born.[190] The Father Brown detective stories first made their appearance in magazines before eventually being published in book form.[191]

1905 was a big year for Chesterton. By this time, he had definitely moved from spiritual seeker to practicing Anglican. This same year, he accepted an invitation to preach at St. Paul's Church, Covent Garden. Frances recorded in her diary of this event: "One of the proudest days of my life.... A crammed church—he was very eloquent and restrained." Gilbert preached again the following week and both sermons were published under the title *Preachers from the Pew*.[192]

In addition, in 1905 Chesterton had published his first book of Christian apologetics entitled *Heretics*.[193] His goal in *Heretics* was to study what he considered to be the mistakes of his contemporaries and so discover what was wrong with modern thought.[194]

The author of another one of C. S. Lewis' "Top Ten," Arthur James Balfour, was very impressed with *Heretics*. When Chesterton and Balfour met at the Synthetic Society, the former found the latter very interesting to talk to, but Balfour appeared bored with the conversation.[195] Maisie Ward's father later wrote rather humorously of this meeting:

> Had you been at the Synthetic last night you would have witnessed a memorable scene.
>
> Place: Westminster Palace Hotel. Time: 9:40.
>
> A. J. B. [Arthur Balfour, leader of the Conservative Party] is speaking persuasively and in carefully modulated tones to an attentive audience. Suddenly a crash as though the door were blown open. A. J. B. brought to a halt. The whole company look round and in rushes a figure exactly like the pictures of Mr. Wind when he blows open the door and forces an entrance in the German child's story "Mr. Wind and Madame Rain"—a figure enormous and distended, a kind of walking mountain but with large rounded corners. It was G. K. C. who, enveloped in a huge Inverness cape of light colour, thus made his debut at the Synthetic.[196]

In 1905, Chesterton published his story collection, *The Club of Queer Trades,* and began writing weekly articles for the *Illustrated London News.* The same year, Chesterton began to publicly debate George Bernard Shaw, an activity that would last for the next thirty years.

In 1906, Chesterton, an adoring fan of Dickens, published his biography of the great novelist.[197] Then in 1908, he had published his second work of Christian apologetics, *Orthodoxy,*[198] along with his novel, *The Man Who Was Thursday,* and a collection of essays entitled *All Things Considered.* Ronald Knox called *The Man Who Was Thursday* "an extraordinary book, written as if the publisher had commissioned him to write something rather like the Pilgrim's Progress in the style of the Pickwick Papers."[199] In the course of *Orthodoxy,* Chesterton referred to the earlier works of John Henry Newman and the Oxford Movement in support of his view of the Anglican position. In the book, he also asserted that he avoided works of Christian apologetics. However, this should not be taken to mean that Chesterton did not read some of the great writers down through church history. Chesterton was asked to draw up a Scheme of Reading for 1908 in *TP's Weekly.* He suggested Butler's *Analogy,* Coleridge's *Confessions of an Enquiring Spirit,* Newman's *Apologia,* St. Augustine's *Confessions,* and the *Summa* of St. Thomas Aquinas.[200]

Orthodoxy, more than any other book, provides us with a history of Chesterton's own thought.[201] In it, Chesterton provides the reader with a number of helpful analogies, some of which Lewis would take up later, such as the analogy of human history being like a play:

> God had written not so much a poem, but rather a play; a play he had

planned as perfect, but which had necessarily been left to human actors and stage-managers who had since made a great mess of it.[202]

Chesterton sold *Orthodoxy* outright for £100. As Maisie Ward later said of this: "No man ever worked so hard to earn so little."[203] Chesterton, like Lewis after him, was a published author for many years before he finally obtained a literary agent who got him better terms on all his book contracts. Chesterton once wrote to his agent, Messrs. A. P. Watt, "The prices you have got me for books, compared with what I used weakly to demand, seem to me to come out of fairyland."[204]

Reading Newman definitely had a profound impact on Chesterton's life and thought. In this regard, Chesterton once wrote,

> A man who is always going back and picking to pieces his own first principles may be having an amusing time but he is not developing as Newman understood development. Newman meant that if you wanted a tree to grow you must plant it finally in some definite spot. It may be (I do not know and I do not care) that Catholic Christianity is just now passing through one of its numberless periods of undue repression and silence. But I do know this, that when the great flowers break forth again, the new epics and the new arts, they will break out on the ancient and living tree. They cannot break out upon the little shrubs that you are always pulling up by the roots to see if they are growing.[205]

In 1909, one of Chesterton's friends, Maurice Baring, became a Roman Catholic. This turn of events would have a decided influence on Chesterton's own spiritual journey. In this same year, Gilbert and his wife Frances moved from Battersea in London to what was then the small country town of Beaconsfield where they would live for the rest of their lives.[206] Today, Beaconsfield is located off the M40 motorway, just beyond the London "beltway" M25, on the way to Oxford. As Chesterton later said in his *Autobiography*: "I have lived in Beaconsfield from the time when it was almost a village, to the time when, as the enemy profanely says, it is a suburb."[207]

The Beaconsfield years saw a stream of works continue to pour forth from Chesterton's pen. In 1909, he published another novel, *The Ball and the Cross*, another biography, this time on George Bernard Shaw, and another essay collection, *Tremendous Trifles*. The following year saw the publication of two more essay collections: *What's Wrong with the World*[208] and *Alarms and Discursions*. In 1911, Chesterton published the first of a series of works for which he would become best known: *The Innocence of Father Brown*, along with a literary critical work on Dickens and two volumes of verse: *Lepanto* and *The Ballad of the White Horse*. Like any author, Chesterton enjoyed receiving praise from his readers. None pleased him more than a note from fellow author John

Buchan written on June 21, 1915, "The other day in the trenches we shouted your Lepanto."[209]

In 1912, Chesterton began to have built "Top Meadow", a studio that would eventually become also a home for him and Frances. The same year Chesterton saw the publication of another novel, *Manalive*, and another collection of essays entitled *A Miscellany of Men*.

Another person close to Chesterton converted to the Catholic Church in 1913; this time it was his brother, Cecil, who would serve and die in The Great War.

By the time of the First World War, Chesterton was quite famous, so much so that even other great authors longed to meet him. H. G. Wells recorded one instance of this:

> I once saw [Henry] James quarrelling with his brother William James, the psychologist. He had lost his calm; he was terribly unnerved. He appealed to me, to me of all people, to adjudicate on what was and what was not permissible in England. William was arguing about it in an indisputably American accent, with an indecently naked reasonableness. I had come to Rye with a car to fetch William James and his daughter to my home at Sandgate. William had none of Henry's passionate regard for the polish upon the surface of life and he was immensely excited by the fact that in the little Rye inn, which had its garden just over the high brick wall of the garden of Lamb House, G. K. Chesterton was staying. William James had corresponded with our vast contemporary and he sorely wanted to see him. So with a scandalous directness he had put the gardener's ladder against that ripe red wall and clambered up and peeped over!
>
> Henry had caught him at it. It was the sort of thing that isn't done. It was most emphatically the sort of thing that isn't done.... Henry instructed the gardener to put away that ladder and William was looking thoroughly naughty about it.
>
> To Henry's manifest relief, I carried William off and in the road just outside the town we ran against the Chestertons who had been for a drive in Romney Marsh; Chesterton was heated and I think rather swollen by the sunshine; he seemed to overhang his one-horse fly; he descended slowly but firmly; he was moist and steamy but cordial; we chatted in the road and William got his coveted impression.[210]

Though Chesterton did not serve in the war, he did fall seriously ill in 1914. The problem was with Chesterton's heart. By the end of the year, he suffered a relapse that left him often unconscious. The illness lasted for months.[211]

Though Chesterton's heart trouble left him tired, and the exhaustion was evident in his writing, still it did not stop or even slow the flow of Chesterton's composition.[212] In the year of his illness, he published *The Wisdom of Father Brown*, another novel, *The Flying Inn*, and a commentary entitled *The Barbarism of Berlin and The Appetite of Tyranny*. Two more commentaries followed, *The Crimes of England* in 1915 and *Eugenics and Other Evils* in 1917. In addition, in 1917 Chesterton published *A Short History of England*. Typical of the man, there are very few dates in his *History*. As always, what Chesterton lacked in facts, he made up for with vision and insight into the essence of great events.[213]

After the signing of the Armistice, Chesterton soon found himself in mourning. His brother Cecil died in hospital in France on December 6, 1918.[214] Despite this great loss, Chesterton and his wife used the opportunity of newfound world peace to travel near and far: to Jerusalem, the Continent and to North America, the latter for a lecture tour.[215] Chesterton, in turn, wrote and published his thoughts on these journeys. *Irish Impressions* came out in 1919, *The New Jerusalem* in 1920 and *What I Saw in America* was published in 1922. During these same years, Chesterton continued to publish in some of the same genres as he had in the past. Another essay collection, *Uses of Diversity*, came out in 1921, and another mystery collection, *The Man Who Knew Too Much*, was published in 1922.

1922 was, perhaps, the most decisive and important of Chesterton's life, for it was in that year that he followed his friend Maurice Baring and his brother Cecil in joining the Catholic Church. One thing that kept Chesterton from joining the Catholic Church for some time was the opinion of his wife Frances. When she made it known that she would not oppose him becoming a Catholic, Chesterton made his move. Frances would eventually follow her husband into the Catholic Church in 1926. Chesterton later wrote that…

> the greatest argument for Catholicism is exactly what makes it so hard to argue for it. It is the scale and multiplicity of the forms of truth and help that it has to offer.[216]

Chesterton's reasons for becoming Catholic may also be summed up in his statement in *The New Witness*: "We do not want, as the newspapers say, a Church that will move with the world. We want a Church that will move the world."[217]

Chesterton's publications after 1922 in many ways reflected this important spiritual change in his life. In 1923, he published a biography of St. Francis of Assisi. In the same year, *Fancies Versus Fads* came into print. Then, in 1925, the book that would be so influential in the life of C. S. Lewis appeared: *The Everlasting Man*. In addition, in 1925, Chesterton published *Wine, Water, and Song: Collected Poems*,[218] *Tales of the Long Bow*, *Superstitions of the Sceptic*, and *William Cobbett*.

1925 also saw the launch of *G. K.'s Weekly*, the newspaper that, in a sense, became the official publication of the Distributist League, an organization founded by Chesterton and Belloc.[219] The *Weekly* was a continuation of the paper started by Gilbert's brother Cecil, *The New Witness*.[220] George Bernard Shaw suggested the new name for the paper.[221] Distributism was an economic policy somewhere between capitalism and communism. It advocated that the ownership of the means of production should be as widely spread as possible among the general populace. Chesterton summed up the Distributist goal by saying, "Their simple idea was to restore possession."[222] Chesterton sought "a return to the sanity of field and workshop, of craftsman and peasant, from the insanity of trusts and machinery, of unemployment, over-production and starvation."[223] Though Chesterton seldom worked in the office of the newspaper, one of his employees said, "You always knew when he was there by the smell of his cigar." Chesterton was a chain smoker and always used the same brand.[224]

The second half of the 1920s saw Chesterton continuing to publish on many topics. In 1926, there was *The Incredulity of Father Brown*, *The Catholic Church and Conversion*, and *The Outline of Sanity*. In 1927, he published *The Secret of Father Brown* and *The Return of Don Quixote*. Another of Chesterton's essay collections came forth from the press in 1928 entitled *Generally Speaking*. Finally, in 1929 *The Poet and the Lunatics*, *The Thing* and *Why I Am a Catholic* came into print.

1929 was also the year of the founding of the Detective Club, a gathering of famous authors of murder mysteries including Chesterton, Agatha Christie and Dorothy Sayers, among others. Chesterton soon became President of the group.[225]

A visit to Rome, also in '29, resulted in another book, *The Resurrection of Rome*. Chesterton even interviewed Mussolini with whom he discussed his own social ideals. Mussolini promised to go away and think over what Chesterton had said, but obviously none of it was taken to heart, let alone action.[226] The meeting that Chesterton valued more on this particular trip was his audience with the Pope. He was so excited by the opportunity that he did no work for two days prior or two days afterwards.[227]

The 1930s witnessed the final flowering of Chesterton's life and career. In 1930, he took a second lecture tour across North America that was highly publicized. The newspapers took special interest in the man's physical size, something of which Chesterton always made a joke. He was reported to be six foot three and three hundred pounds.[228] However, when asked, Chesterton said he was actually six foot two inches and that his weight could never be accurately calculated.[229] The greatest difficulty of the trip was getting Chesterton in and out of various motor vehicles.[230]

In 1932, he began regular BBC broadcasts on literary topics, a harbinger of Lewis' own radio talks.

> The radio suited him so excellently, precisely because it is a personal sitting down man to man relationship that the successful broadcaster must establish; that was the relationship inside which he naturally thought.[231]

Then in 1934, the Pope named Chesterton Knight Commander with Star in the Order of St. Gregory the Great. The honor was shared with Chesterton's friend, Hilaire Belloc.[232]

Literary pieces continued to find their way into print during Chesterton's final years: *Four Faultless Felons* (1930), *The Resurrection of Rome* (1930), *Come to Think of It* (1931), *Chaucer* (1932), *St. Thomas Aquinas* (1933), *All I Survey* (1933), *Avowals and Denials* (1934), *The Scandal of Father Brown* (1935), and *The Well and the Shallows* (1935). Though critics complained of Chesterton writing on topics on which he was not an expert, such as Chaucer, GKC continued to argue for the rights of the amateur.[233] Nonetheless, some scholars, like Etienne Gilson, found great value in Chesterton's work. Gilson's admiration for Chesterton began with *Greybeards at Play* and he thought *Orthodoxy* "the best piece of apologetic the century has produced." Gilson called Chesterton's volume on Aquinas "the best book ever written on St. Thomas."[234]

Appropriately enough, the final volume Chesterton prepared for the press was his own *Autobiography* first published in 1936. Gilbert Keith Chesterton died of heart failure on June 14 of that year.[235] He was 62 years old and had over one hundred published titles to his credit. In the memorial service that took place in Westminster Cathedral a telegram from Cardinal Pacelli, who later became Pope Pius XII, was read:

> Holy Father deeply grieved death Mr. Gilbert Keith Chesterton devoted son Holy Church gifted Defender of the Catholic Faith. His Holiness offers paternal sympathy people of England assures prayers dear departed, bestows Apostolic Benediction.[236]

LEWIS' TOP TEN

The Everlasting Man : A Synopsis

In many ways, this book is Chesterton's response to a volume written by a friend and sparring partner: H. G. Wells' *The Outline of History* published in 1920. The book is divided into two parts, Part I: On the Creature Called Man, and Part II: On the Man Called Christ. Chesterton's thesis is that...

> ... those who say that Christ stands side by side with similar myths, and his religion side by side with similar religions, are only repeating a very stale formula contradicted by a very striking fact.[237]

Introduction
Chesterton begins by saying that:

> There are two ways of getting home; and one of them is to stay there. The other is to walk round the whole world till we come back to the same place.[238]

Chesterton goes on to suggest that the next best thing to being inside Christendom is to be really outside of it. As a friend of mine once said, "Every few years we need to forget everything we think we know about Jesus and start fresh." Chesterton may not have agreed that we need to conduct this experiment every year, but he certainly would have agreed that we need to try it at least once. We need to recover the "candour and wonder" of the child and pretend we are hearing the Christian story for the first time.

Priests and ministers are confronted with this challenge every Sunday: it is difficult to make the colors of Christianity vivid because they are so familiar. Chesterton suggests that perhaps we should tell the story of Christ as though he were a Chinese hero. Call him the Son of Heaven instead of the Son of God. Maybe then we would:

> ...admire the chivalry of the Chinese conception of a god who fell from the sky to fight the dragons and save the wicked from being devoured by their own fault and folly.[239]

Lewis attempted what Chesterton suggests here on more than one occasion. The first book Lewis wrote as a Christian, *The Pilgrim's Regress*, is, in a sense, the story of a man who travels around the world and back again in order to find his home. In his Cosmic Trilogy, Lewis tried to capture the strangeness of the Christian story by telling it from an otherworldly perspective. Then of course in *The Chronicles of Narnia*, Lewis re-imagines the Christian story in a land of talking beasts. Lewis himself did exactly what Chesterton suggests in his own life: he got completely outside Christendom and only then did he begin to understand it. Lewis felt his first arrival in Oxford offered a metaphor of his life. He turned the wrong way out of the railway station and began walking away from the center of the city. Only after he had walked a couple of miles did he turn around and see that "sweet city with her dreaming spires". Sometimes we do need to get completely outside of something to understand it; we need to step back and take in the big picture. Chesterton and Lewis are both good guides, assisting us in our round-the-world journey home.

Part I: On the Creature Called Man

The Man in the Cave

Chesterton opens this chapter by saying:

> Far away in some strange constellation in skies infinitely remote, there is a small star, which astronomers may some day discover. At least I could never observe in the faces or demeanour of most astronomers or men of science any evidence that they have discovered it; though as a matter of fact they were walking about on it all the time. It is a star that brings forth out of itself very strange plants and very strange animals; and none stranger than the men of science.[240]

Thus, Chesterton begins his attack against science, or at least against, what Lewis later called, "scientism". By scientism Lewis meant:

> A certain outlook on the world which is casually connected with the popularization of the sciences, though it is much less common among real scientists than among their readers.[241]

Chesterton's main point in this chapter seems to be a questioning of the idea of human evolution. He says,

> Nobody can imagine how nothing could turn into something. Nobody can get an inch nearer to it by explaining how something could turn into something else.[242]

Chesterton admits that human beings have "a backbone or other parts upon a similar pattern to birds and fishes", but he questions the meaning of this fact.[243] He also admits that: "There may be a broken trail of stones and bones faintly suggesting the development of the human body." However, Chesterton maintains that: "There is nothing even faintly suggesting such a development of the human mind."[244] Chesterton refers to Pithecanthropus, the name given by Eugene Dubois to a creature intermediate in its evolutionary position between apes and humans. Dubois discovered the skullcap and femur of Pithecanthropus in Southeast Asia in 1891.[245] One of Chesterton's major points in this chapter is that "Art is the signature of man."[246]

Pithecanthropus did not draw a reindeer badly and Homo Sapiens draw it well. The higher animals did not draw better and better portraits; the dog did not paint better in his best period than in his early bad manner as a jackal; the wild horse was not an Impressionist and the race-horse a Post-Impressionist. All we can say of this notion of reproducing things in shadow or representative shape is that it exists nowhere in nature except in man; and that we cannot even talk about it without treating man as something separate from nature.[247]

It is doubtful that Lewis was much influenced by Chesterton in his views on evolution. Lewis himself was much more accepting of the biological theory of evolution than Chesterton ever was. [248]

Professors and Prehistoric Men

In this chapter, Chesterton continues to question the idea of human evolution. He doubts whether human evolution is something that scientists can tell us accurately about at all, for a scientist "cannot watch the Missing Link evolving in his own backyard."[249] According to Chesterton, the problem is not with Darwin but the dogmatism of Darwinians.

> They talk of searching for the habitat of the Missing Link; as if one were to talk of being on friendly terms with the gap in a narrative or the hole in an argument, of taking a walk with a *non-sequitur* or dining with an undistributed middle.[250]

Chesterton admits that man's body may have evolved from the brutes but we know nothing of a similar evolution of the soul.[251] We know nothing of prehistoric human beings simply because they were prehistoric and therefore, by definition, left no written record of their existence.[252] According to Chesterton, we cannot be certain that Pithecanthropus ever worshiped because we cannot be certain that such a being ever lived.[253]

Chesterton asserts that one of the earliest things we can know of human existence is that it took shape in the trinity of the family: father, mother and child. This ancient trinity foreshadows a newer trinity, that of the Holy Family consisting of child and mother and father.[254]

The Antiquity of Civilization

Chesterton continues his outline of human history in this chapter by reiterating his commitment to a sort of anthropological agnosticism about the first human beings. He doubts that Mr. H. G. Wells knows as much about "the Old Man" as he thinks or says he knows. According to Chesterton, we cannot base our understanding of ancient humanity upon the study of savage tribes in the twentieth century: "But the despotism in certain dingy and decayed tribes in the twentieth century does not prove that the first men were ruled despotically."[255]

Our knowledge of primitive humanity is, at best, imperfect. This is true, says Chesterton, because the curtain rises on the play of human history already in progress. The most ancient records "take for granted things like kings and priests and princes and assemblies of the people."[256] The first chapters of the human story have been torn out of the book and we shall never read them. However, when it comes to the first written records that we do have, Chesterton thinks it overwhelmingly probable that ancient priests were the ones who invented the art of writing.[257]

In his survey of ancient civilization, Chesterton focuses on Egypt and Babylon. He definitely gives pride of place to those ancient civilizations that eventually gave birth to modern Western civilization. Chesterton even goes so far as to say: "with all respect to the Aztecs and the Mongols of the Far East, they did not matter as the Mediterranean tradition mattered and still matters."[258] Why does Mediterranean tradition matter most? Chesterton does not flinch from giving the answer:

> When all is said, if there were nothing in the world but what was said and done and written and built in the lands lying round the Mediterranean, it would still be in all the most vital and valuable things to the world in which we live. When that southern culture spread to the north-west it produced many very wonderful things; of which doubtless we ourselves are the most wonderful.[259]

Despite Chesterton's Euro-centrism and Euro-hubris which seem almost unforgiveable, the twenty-first century reader of *The Everlasting Man* should still be able to appreciate the way in which Chesterton waxes eloquent about the Greek tradition:

> A poet who may have been a beggar and a ballad-monger, who may have been unable to read and write, and was described by tradition as blind, composed a poem about the Greeks going to war with this town to recover the most beautiful woman in the world.... It is said that the poem came at the end of the period; that the primitive culture brought it forth in its decay; in which case one would like to have seen that culture in its prime.... If the world becomes pagan and perishes, the last man left alive would do well to quote the Iliad and die.[260]

God and Comparative Religion

In this chapter, Chesterton asserts that the only real rival to Christianity is Paganism, something "almost native and normal to the great fellowship we call mankind."[261] Intriguingly, Chesterton denies that Confucianism and

Buddhism are even religions.[262] Islam he calls an imitation of Christianity, but hardly the same thing.[263] Chesterton finds no common character between Christianity, Islam, Confucianism, and Buddhism, nor does he find anything in common between their founders: Christ, Mohammed, Buddha, and Confucius.[264] Christianity is unique just as the Jews are unique among peoples of the world, for they belong to an ancient culture yet are scattered among the nations as a distinct people.[265]

Chesterton argues for the belief that religion began with monotheism and that polytheism developed from this. The only reason this is not usually acknowledged is that evolutionists are used to focusing on the idea that trees come from seeds, whereas at the same time they fail to focus on the truth that seeds come from trees.[266] This is a Chestertonian idea that C. S. Lewis later picks up and develops.[267] Chesterton offers the Australian aborigines as an example of a primitive people holding to monotheism.[268]

However, what of the Jews? Where do they fit in Chesterton's examination of God and Comparative Religion? Chesterton speaks of the Jewish journey through history as a "romance of restlessness". The important thing about Judaism is that it preserved the idea of the one God above all gods for the world. It was essential that this God have no image since Judaism arose in a land of monstrous gods, Moloch and Dagon among them. Moreover, there are things in the tradition of Israel that belong to all humanity now, such as the book of Job, which Chesterton calls one of the colossal cornerstones of the world.[269]

Chesterton's comparison, or lack of comparison really, of various religions will probably only be convincing to those who already hold Christian presuppositions. Chesterton ends his breezy overview precisely where he began:

> It is really the collapse of comparative religion that there is no comparison between God and the gods. There is no more comparison than there is between a man and the men who walked about in his dreams.[270]

Nonetheless, Chesterton hovers in this chapter around an idea that will become very important to Lewis: that in pagan religion we have a foreshadowing of Christ. Even Lewis' beloved Virgil provides such a foretaste: "Virgil spoke to all who suffer with the veritable cry of a Christian before Christ: 'O you that have borne things more terrible, to this also God shall give an end.'"[271]

Man and Mythologies
In this chapter, Chesterton re-iterates the point that will become so

important to C. S. Lewis: that all the mythologies of the world are "daydreams".[272] "The pagans had dreams about realities."[273] "We may truly call these foreshadowings." "These things [mythologies] were something *like* the real thing."[274] Lewis' friends, J. R. R. Tolkien and Hugo Dyson, pick up this point in a conversation with Lewis in 1931 and help him to see that the story of Christ is a true myth.[275]

Chesterton touches on themes that often stirred Lewis' subconscious, but Chesterton suggests that to which these themes might be pointing. Chesterton's very way of putting things in this chapter foreshadow Lewis' own. For example, Chesterton says:

> Suppose somebody in a story says 'Pluck this flower and a princess will die in a castle beyond the sea,' we do not know why something stirs in the subconsciousness, or why what is impossible seems almost inevitable.[276]

Lewis uses almost identical language forty years later in *Letters to Malcolm: Chiefly on Prayer*. In speaking of Holy Communion, Lewis writes:

> When I say "magic" I am not thinking of the paltry and pathetic techniques by which fools attempt and quacks pretend to control nature. I mean rather what is suggested by fairy-tale sentences like "This is a magic flower, and if you carry it the seven gates will open to you of their own accord"...[277]

Chesterton asserts that the person who has no sympathy with myths has no sympathy with humanity. On the other hand, the person who sympathizes most with mythology will realize that it satisfies only one aspect of our humanity, namely the imaginative aspect. Mythologies are not religions, for they lack a creed.[278] Paganism itself, Chesterton says, is the attempt to reach the divine through the imagination.[279] However, human beings have reason as well as imagination, and reason is not satisfied with mythology. Rather, reason is operative in philosophy. Furthermore, philosophy and mythology are like rivers running parallel to one another until they meet in the sea of Christianity. The Church is the first entity to combine reason and religion, Chesterton maintains.[280] All of this must have spoken rather powerfully to C. S. Lewis, who struggled his whole life to unite the reasoning and imaginative sides of his personality.

The Demons and the Philosophers

At the beginning of this chapter, Chesterton divides human history into four stages:

1. Imaginative Paganism

2. The struggle between Paganism and something less worthy
3. The degeneration of Paganism
4. Christendom

Chesterton summarizes the degeneration of Paganism in this manner: there is a weakness in polytheism, the weakness of original sin. The pagan gods are depicted as tossing men like dice. Furthermore, the sex-obsession of the gods, paralleling the sex-obsession of humans, dragged down the winged fancies of paganism.

The "something less worthy" than Paganism that Chesterton summarizes in this chapter is devil worship. Superstition is a part of this and superstition recurs in all ages, even or especially, in rationalistic ones.[281] However, the real question, Chesterton says, is whether the various spirits will answer when called upon. He asserts that some sort of desperate impulse has driven human beings down through the ages to call upon dark powers when dealing with very practical problems.[282] Historically speaking, the cult of the demons follows after the cult of the gods, even after the cult of one, single God. The demons have been in hiding since the coming of Christ, but some of the highest civilizations have exalted Satan in the form of human sacrifice (ie. the Aztecs, the Native Americans, Carthage). The Christian is worse off than these civilizations in only one sense: that he or she ought to know better.[283]

In the second half of this chapter, Chesterton discusses those whom he calls "the Philosophers". Under this heading, he deals mainly with: Aristotle, Plato, Confucius, Akenahten, and Buddha. Aristotle he calls the greatest and most practical of all philosophers, the one who anticipated most fully the sacramental sanity of the Church. Plato anticipated Catholic realism by insisting that ideas are realities.

Chesterton calls Confucius an agnostic who dealt mainly with morals, not theology or philosophy per se. He was not a prophet bringing a message from heaven but a man organizing China. Akenahten, as Pharaoh, was a royal philosopher who hurled down the high gods of Egypt and modeled a type of monotheism by lifting up the sun as the focus of worship.

Chesterton spends the majority of this section of this chapter discussing "the Lord Buddha," a few pages in fact. He believes that Buddhism is best viewed as a philosophy, not a religion. Buddha he calls the greatest and best of the royal philosophers. He was a philosopher who founded a school of philosophy and was later turned into a type of divinity. The most important thing that Buddha did was to develop a metaphysical discipline for eradicating desire: the cause of all human sorrow. However, to Chesterton's mind this "ecstasy of indifference" is indistinguishable from despair. All religious history is a series of noughts and crosses, a series of negatives compared to the positive shape of Christianity. The temptation of the philosophers has been to propound explanations of the universe that are too obvious compared to the common sense reality of Christianity. One of these too obvious explanations is that of Buddhism, that everything is a dream or delusion. Another is that all things recur. A third is that nothing will be right with the world until we as individuals are melted again into a single unity.[284]

The War of the Gods and Demons

This chapter deals with the war between paganism and "something less worthy than paganism", between Rome and Carthage.

> There is a religious war when two worlds meet; that is, when two visions of the world meet; or in more modern language when two moral atmospheres meet. What is the one man's breath is the other man's poison; and it is vain to talk of giving a pestilence a place in the sun. And this is what we must understand, even at the expense of digression, if we would see what really happened in the Mediterranean; when right athwart the rising of the Republic on the Tiber, a thing overtopping and disdaining it, dark with all the riddles of Asia and trailing all the tribes and dependencies of imperialism, came Carthage riding on the sea.[285]

Chesterton maintains that these two spirits are still abroad in the world today: the spirit of Carthage and the spirit of Rome, the materialist on one hand and the supernaturalist on the other.

> It may sound fanciful to say that men we meet at tea-tables or talk to at garden-parties are secretly worshippers of Baal or Moloch. But this sort of commercial mind has its own cosmic vision and it is the vision of Carthage. It has in it the brutal blunder that was the ruin of Carthage. The Punic power fell, because there is in this materialism a mad indifference to real thought. By disbelieving in the soul, it comes to disbelieving in the mind.[286]

According to Chesterton, we can thank God, or our lucky stars, that we are descendants of Rome and not of Carthage, for Rome testifies to the sanity that is the soul of Europe. The struggle that established Christendom would have been very different if it had been fought within a Carthaginian empire instead of a Roman one. As history turned out, divine things descended upon a human construct and not an inhuman one. According to Chesterton, we can be grateful that Rome kept heathenry human.[287]

The End of the World

Chesterton begins this chapter with the story of an acquaintance of his:

Louis de Rougement. Chesterton asserts that he does not believe, with de Rougement, that mythology must begin with eroticism. However, he does believe that all mythology, gone to seed as it were, ends up there.[288]

> There comes an hour in the afternoon when the child is tired of 'pretending'; when he is weary of being a robber or a Red Indian. It is then that he torments the cat. There comes a time in the routine of an ordered civilization when the man is tired of playing at mythology and pretending that a tree is a maiden or that the moon made love to a man. The effect of this staleness is the same everywhere; it is seen in all drug-taking and dram-drinking and every form of the tendency to increase the dose. Men seek stranger sins or more startling obscenities as stimulants to their jaded sense. They seek after mad oriental religions for the same reason. They try to stab their nerves to life, as if it were with the knives of the priests of Baal. They are walking in their sleep and try to wake themselves up with nightmares.[289]

Chesterton sees this as the problem of ancient Greece. It allowed a perversion to become a convention. Chesterton presents what he believes to be a truism:

> Let any lad who has had the luck to grow up sane and simple in his day-dreams of love hear for the first time of the cult of Ganymede; he will not be merely shocked but sickened.[290]

However, according to Chesterton, the good news is that Rome triumphed over Greece just as it won out over Carthage. He admits that Virgil sometimes takes over a theme from Theocritus, one of the first voices in the homoerotic pastoral tradition.[291] However, Chesterton concludes: "Nobody who reads even a few lines of Virgil can doubt that he understood what moral sanity means to mankind."[292] Virgil's genius is that he took something from Homer and created out of it...

> ... a legend of the almost divine dignity that belongs to the defeated. This was one of the traditions that did truly prepare the world for the coming of Christianity and especially of Christian chivalry.

The other element of genius that Chesterton sees in Virgil is that he is concerned with the "*numina* of natural and agricultural life". Chesterton draws from Virgil the principle that "the conventions of complex cities were less really healthy and happy than the customs of the countryside."[293] Lewis certainly agreed with this. He loved the countryside of County Down, Oxfordshire, and all of rural Ireland and England far more than he liked the city. Even Lewis' picture of heaven in *The Great Divorce* is a rural scene and not a city as in the biblical book of *Revelation*.

Another point that Chesterton asserts in this passage that would become very important to Lewis and to Lewis' conversion in particular, is that Christianity is the true fulfillment of paganism:

> It is said truly that Pan died because Christ was born. It is almost as true in another sense that men knew that Christ was born because Pan was already dead. A void was made by the vanishing of the whole mythology of mankind, which would have asphyxiated like a vacuum if it had not been filled with theology.[294]

According to Chesterton, just as paganism was dying out to make way for its fulfillment in Christ, so also philosophy was stalling out to make way for the Logos. The life of the great Greek civilization, taken over by Rome, was going on with "dreary industry and festivity". It was the end of the world, but an end that was making way for a new beginning.[295]

Part II: On the Man Called Christ

The God in the Cave

As he begins Part II of this book, Chesterton takes us back to the cave. However, this time it is not the Man in the Cave whom we are examining, it is God in the cave. Chesterton points out how Jesus, the God-Man, was born in a cave where animals were stabled. Christ being born in a cave marked him out as a homeless outcast. One of the amazing things about this birth is that it brought heaven to a place under the earth.[296] Chesterton rings the changes on this theme, ringing the Christmas bells as it were. In fact, this entire chapter, read aloud, would make an excellent Christmas sermon.

At the center of the Christmas story is an event that contains an idea with powerful theological and psychological implications. The Christmas event contains two ideas that most of humankind would consider quite remote from each other: "the idea of a baby and the idea of unknown strength that sustains the stars".[297]

From this point on through the rest of the chapter, Chesterton takes several of the characters in the Christmas story and explores the deeper meaning that he sees behind each one. He begins with the Blessed Virgin Mary. He says that he could never imagine, at any stage in his development, the reason why respect paid to Mary was controversial. He recalls a controversy in his parish church when he was a boy over a statue representing Mary and Jesus. Some wanted the statue removed; some wanted it to remain. They compromised by removing the baby, but not Mary. Chesterton sees in this a parable. You cannot chip away at the statue of a mother all around a newborn child, nor can you suspend the sculpture of a baby in mid air. One cannot visit the child without visiting the mother. Chesterton notes that:

> ...the notion of a hero appearing, like Pallas from the brain of Zeus, mature and without a mother, is obviously the very opposite of the idea of a god being born like an ordinary baby and entirely dependent on a mother.[298]

Next, Chesterton looks at the Shepherds. Part of the significance of the birth of Christ being announced to them is that they were the lowest of the low. They were among the people of the land. Chesterton sees in this event the beginning of the end of slavery.[299] Peasants, like these shepherds, were also the makers of mythology.

> Everywhere else Arcadia was fading from the forest. Pan was dead and the shepherds were scattered like sheep. And though no man knew it, the hour was near which was to end and to fulfill all things; and though no man heard it, there was one far-off cry in an unknown tongue upon the heaving wilderness of the mountains. The shepherds had found their Shepherd.[300]

In the coming of the wise men to worship the Christ child, Chesterton sees something like Confucius, Pythagoras, and Plato bowing down in humble recognition of that for which they had dimly longed.

> Confucius would have found a new foundation for the family in the very reversal of the Holy Family. Buddha would have looked upon a new renunciation, of stars rather than jewels and divinity than royalty. Buddha would have come from his impersonal paradise to worship a person. Confucius would have come from his temples of ancestor-worship to worship a child.[301]

In the wise men coming to worship the Christ child, they each found something larger than their own philosophies. In the same way, Chesterton sees the Catholic faith as something truly universal, large enough to contain the truths of all other religions and philosophies. Yet, in another way, worshiping the Christ requires a renunciation. The early Christians were invited to set up the image of Jesus alongside that of Jupiter, Mithras, Osiris, Atys, and Ammon, but they refused, and that refusal was the turning point of history. Mythology came with the shepherds, philosophy came with the wise men, and each found their fulfillment, so to speak, in the cave where God was born.[302]

The final character in the Christmas story that Chesterton examines is Herod. The king who felt the "earthquake under him and swayed with his swaying palace".[303]

Herod had his place, therefore, in the miracle play of Bethlehem because he is the menace to the Church Militant and shows it from the first as under persecution and fighting for its life.[304]

In summary, Chesterton sees three key ideas in the Christmas story:

1. The human poetic instinct for a heaven that is as local as a home, typified in the shepherds.
2. The human philosophical desire for a philosophy larger than all other philosophies, typified in the wise men.
3. A challenge and a fight, typified in the character of Herod.

Other religions may have one or two of these elements, but not all three. That is why, according to Chesterton, the story of Christmas has such a hold on the imagination.[305]

The Riddles of the Gospel

Chesterton begins this chapter by pointing out the argument that serves as the backbone of his book. This argument follows the form of *reductio ad absurdum* and assumes that the results of following the rationalist thesis are more irrational than the Christian thesis. In Part I, Chesterton treats humankind as merely an animal and thus reveals how preposterous an outlook this is. In Part II, he sets out the view that Christ was merely human and thus shows how ridiculous the notion is.

In this chapter in particular, Chesterton tries to imagine what a non-Christian, reading the Gospels for the first time, would think about them. Would such a reader find in Jesus merely a humane lover of humanity? Chesterton suggests there is much more to the figure of Christ in the Gospels than this. There are a great many mysterious aspects to the story of Jesus. For example: why are the Gospels silent about the circumstances of Jesus' life from age twelve to thirty? Lewis and Chesterton both suggest that a person or a group of people concocting a legend would not allow such a silence to stand. In fact, the later Gnostic Gospels try to fill in this blank, but not the earlier canonical Gospels of the New Testament.

Another strange thing that a neutral observer might note about the Gospels is that, unlike every other moralist down through the centuries, Jesus utters no platitudes. Instead, Jesus makes such unusual statements as: "The meek shall inherit the earth." So-called "freethinkers" often assert that Jesus was a man of his time and that therefore his ethics, for example on marriage, are not conducive to our own time. Chesterton asserts that the data of the Gospels suggest that Jesus was a person from beyond time, rather than a man of his own time. Exactly how suitable Jesus' ideas were to his own time is suggested by the fact that the people of his time crucified him.

Yes, Jesus believed in certain things and practiced certain things, such as healing and exorcism, which the modern materialist rejects. However,

Chesterton suggests, the burden of proof is upon the materialist to prove the impossibility of miracles against the testimony of all humanity.

In summary, Chesterton asserts that a person reading the Gospels objectively would not get the impression of a human Christ. Too many of these human Christs have been put forward by the rationalists for any one of them to be correct. These "rational" explanations of the Gospel may be enumerated as follows. That the Christ of the Gospels was:

1. Merely a myth and that he never really lived.
2. An ethical teacher like one of the Essenes.
3. A madman with a Messianic delusion.
4. The original teacher of Socialism or Pacifism.
5. An apocalyptic prophet.
6. A spiritual healer and nothing else.
7. An exorcist and nothing else.

Chesterton concludes: "There must surely have been something not only mysterious but many-sided about Christ if so many smaller Christs can be carved out of him."[306]

Chesterton finishes this chapter with a statement bordering on the trilemma later echoed by Lewis:

> On the contrary, stumbling on that rock of scandal is the first step. Stark staring incredulity is a far more loyal tribute to that truth than a modernist metaphysic that would make it out merely a matter of degree. It were better to rend our robes with a great cry against blasphemy, like Caiaphas in the judgment, or to lay hold of the man as a maniac possessed of devils like the kinsmen and the crowd, rather than to stand stupidly debating the fine shades of pantheism in the presence of so catastrophic a claim. There is more of the wisdom that is one with surprise in any simple person, full of the sensitiveness of simplicity, who should expect the grass to wither and the birds to drop dead out of the air, when a strolling carpenter's apprentice said calmly and almost carelessly, like one looking over his shoulder: 'Before Abraham was, I am.'[307]

The Strangest Story in the World

Chesterton begins this chapter by noting that his purpose in the last chapter was to stress the divine nature of Christ, an idea, he says, "has been swamped in cheap generalizations".[308] Regarding Christ's human nature, Chesterton asserts that Christ "was more human than a human being was then likely to be."[309] For example, there is what Chesterton calls Christ's literary style dramatically displayed in such parables as the one about the lilies of the field . . . .

> And why take ye thought for raiment? Consider the lilies of the field, how they grow; they toil not, neither do they spin: and yet I say unto you, That even Solomon in all his glory was not arrayed like one of these. Wherefore, if God so clothe the grass of the field, which to day is, and to morrow is cast into the oven, *shall he* not much more *clothe* you, O ye of little faith? (Matthew 6:28 KJV)

Regarding this parable, Chesterton states:

> There is nothing that really indicates a subtle and in the true sense a superior mind so much as this power of comparing a lower thing with a higher and yet that higher with a higher still; of thinking on three planes at once.[310]

This ability to think on three levels at once is the last thing one would associate with a mind dominated by megalomania. This intellectual ability does not prove the divinity of Christ but it is evidence, Chesterton asserts, of distaste for "vainglorious claims to divinity".

On the other hand, Chesterton points out the unlikelihood that Christ did not claim divinity and that the Church made up this claim.

> Even if the Church had mistaken his meaning, it would still be true that no other historical tradition except the Church had ever even made the same mistake. Mahomedans did not misunderstand Mahomet and suppose he was Allah. Jews did not misinterpret Moses and identify him with Jehovah. Why was this claim alone exaggerated unless this alone was made? Even if Christianity was one vast universal blunder, it is still a blunder as solitary as the Incarnation.[311]

Chesterton admits that there are human beings in the world who claim to be divine but are not. However, those kinds of people are usually in lunatic asylums. No one really believes that Jesus was that sort of person. How could the man who preached the Sermon on the Mount be such a "horrible half-witted imbecile"?[312]

Next, Chesterton takes up the question: could Jesus really have been simply a wandering philosopher? Well, if he was, his life seemed to have a much more specific goal or objective—to go to the cross. Chesterton takes a few pages to explore the meaning of Christ's passion. Then he concludes by saying:

> Since that day it has never been quite enough to say that God is in his heaven and all is right with the world; since the rumour that God had left his heavens to set it right.[313]

Chesterton notes how on the cross, "God had been forsaken by God."

Lewis echoes this line in *A Grief Observed*. "Sometimes it is hard not to say, 'God forgive God.' Sometimes it is hard to say so much. But if our faith is true, He didn't. He crucified Him."[314]

After spending pages of discussion on the Passion, Chesterton concludes this chapter with one brief paragraph about the resurrection.[315] The Christian theologian may find this to be wholly insufficient attention to one of the most important events and doctrines of our faith. However, Lewis does not even devote a paragraph to the resurrection in *Mere Christianity*. He skips over the subject altogether.

The Witness of the Heretics

Chesterton begins this chapter with a reference to Jesus' promise to Peter in Matthew 16:18-19…

> And I tell you that you are Peter, and on this rock I will build my church, and the gates of Hades will not overcome it. I will give you the keys of the kingdom of heaven; whatever you bind on earth will be bound in heaven, and whatever you loose on earth will be loosed in heaven.

This is one of those places in *The Everlasting Man* where Chesterton makes no bones about his commitment to the Catholic Church, a commitment that Lewis never accepted for himself. However, Chesterton focuses here not on Peter as the Rock on which the Church is built, but upon the image of the keys of the kingdom. The Early Christian, he says, was a person carrying a key that could unlock the prison of the world and that key was the creed. The creed was like a key in at least three ways:

1. It had a definite and unchanging shape, unlike evolutionism.
2. It had a fantastic shape, something un-guessed, that either fits the lock of the prison of this world or does not.
3. It had an elaborate pattern that unlocks the maze of prisons that humanity had gotten into.

Chesterton, like Lewis after him, utilizes what J. I. Packer has called "a brilliant welter of arguments, stories and evocative illustrations." Thus, Chesterton turns quickly from the image of a key to that of a tree. He maintains that Christianity appeared very rapidly as a full-grown tree. The Church is certainly like a Christmas tree. However, turning almost by free association from the holiday of Christmas to that of Hanukah, Chesterton asserts that early Christianity was as ritualistic as the seven-branched candlestick, or Menorah. Catholic Chesterton cannot imagine why anyone who accepts the Bethlehem tradition should reject the golden or gilded ornament of the Church, since the Magi themselves brought a gift of gold to the Christ Child.

Furthermore, Christianity, even in her earliest form, was certainly a Church, not a "moral movement of idealists".[316]

Chesterton maintains that the Christian faith was not a simple thing growing up in a simple age. Rather, the Church had to be simultaneously Jewish, Greek, Roman, African, and Asian. She had to be, like Paul, all things to all people.[317] The Church did not arise naturally out of the decay of the Roman Empire. Nor was the Church a mere reaction to that decadence. Rather, Manichaeism was the reaction and the Church was the cure. "Now the curious fact is this; that the very heresies which the early Church is blamed for crushing testify to the unfairness for which she is blamed."[318] The Church did not have a hatred of the body, a horror of the material universe, or a suicide of the senses. The Manicheans embodied all these, and the Church condemned the heresy of Mani.[319] The Church answered heresy with dogmatic definitions, for example: declaring that humans are sinful, not that life itself is evil. If the Church had not insisted on theology, she would have "melted into a mad mythology of the mystics".[320]

Another heresy that Chesterton addresses in this chapter is that of Arius (c. 250-c. 336) who maintained that "there was a time when the Son was not."[321] Athanasius rose up against Arius as a maintainer of orthodoxy. Athanasius' efforts led to the formation of the Nicene Creed. Chesterton utilizes this bit of history to make a modern point. He says that if there is one thing modern liberals like to put forward as an example of pure and simple Christianity it is the statement: "God is love." However, one cannot truly make this statement without the Trinity of the Creed. Otherwise, who was there for God to love before creation?[322]

In sum, Chesterton asserts that Christianity was not a collapse into asceticism, nor the shadow of the Empire, nor a panic of hell-fire, nor a Semitic secret society. The witness of the heretics is that Christianity is something much more than any of the heresies. There is no explanation for the Church, holds Chesterton, than "that, like Pallas from the brain of Jove, it had indeed come forth out of the mind of God, mature and mighty and armed for judgment and for war."[323]

The Escape from Paganism

Chesterton begins this chapter with the image of the missionary—an image that he says was often made fun of in his own day. Christian missionaries were looked down upon for thinking their religion was superior to others. However, how could they not think their religion superior when they were ministering to cannibals? Chesterton says that missionaries in his day were criticized for generalizing too much about non-Christians and lumping them all into one category. However, according to Chesterton, the outer world to which the missionary brings his creed really is something subject to certain generalities.[324]

To what generalities is Chesterton referring? He points out that in ancient Greek and Roman culture, religion was one thing and philosophy another. The philosophers did not believe in the gods, nor did the priests sacrificing in the temples show any interest in philosophy. Chesterton puts forward that the same thing is true regarding non-Christian civilization today.

> Eastern paganism really is much more all of a piece, just as ancient paganism was much more all of a piece, than the modern critics admit. It is a many-coloured Persian Carpet as the other was a varied and tessellated Roman pavement; but the one real crack right across that pavement came from the earthquake of the Crucifixion.[325]

Christianity is the only thing that brings religion and philosophy, temple ritual and ethics, together. Chesterton quotes a professor of Persian as saying, "You will never understand oriental religions, because you always conceive religion as connected with ethics. This kind has really nothing to do with ethics."[326]

To Chesterton's mind, Asia stands as the one representative of paganism and the rival of Christianity. If the Church had not come along and transformed Europe, then she would be as Asia is now.[327] Today's reader can be forgiven for being a bit impatient with Chesterton's over-generalizations in this chapter, as well as being put off by his euro-centrism. However, as we shall soon see, there is a point, perhaps a sensible one, that becomes important to Lewis' spiritual journey.

What of Islam as a rival to Christianity? Chesterton recognizes Islam as such. However, Islam is not pre-Christian and therefore, by definition, not pagan. Islam is a product of Christianity, picking up certain common points from its predecessor and developing those points in different ways.[328]

What Christianity brought into the world that the world was lacking was simply hope. The mythologies and the philosophies of the ancient world, Chesterton suggests, were all sad. Even Buddhism, for all its charity, lacks the hope of Christianity, the hope of real change. Only a faith that gives sufficient ground for human free will, as Christianity does, can be a religion of hope.[329] The Christian doctrine of salvation suggests that human life can be like a sculpting project—a project of rejecting certain stones in order to make a beautiful statue, "a victory with wings".[330]

The Catholic faith, says Chesterton, addresses this innate human need for freedom; it also addresses the need for reconciliation between mythology and philosophy. Christianity is a story, like a mythology, only it is a true story. Christianity is also a philosophy, but it is the one most true to real life. However, more important is the fact that Christianity brings these two together; it provides a philosophy of stories. All other philosophies ignore the human instinct to write fairy tales, but not Christianity. In fact, Christianity brings together various types of story: the tale, the test, the adventure, and the ordeal of the free person.[331]

> To sum up; the sanity of the world was restored and the soul of man offered salvation by something which did indeed satisfy the two warring tendencies of the past; which had never been satisfied in full and most certainly never satisfied together.... If there be indeed a God, his creation could hardly have reached any other culmination than this granting of a real romance to the world. Otherwise the two sides of the human mind could never have touched at all; and the brain of man would have remained cloven and double; one lobe of it dreaming impossible dreams and the other repeating invariable calculations.[332]

Thus, Christianity satisfies both the left-brain and the right-brain. This is something C. S. Lewis sought throughout his life: a reconciliation of the imaginative and logical sides of his mind. We see this battle and reconciliation depicted in such works as *Till We Have Faces*.

This is, perhaps, the point at which *The Everlasting Man* helped Lewis the most. In *Surprised by Joy* he writes:

> Paganism had been only the childhood of religion, or only a prophetic dream. Where was the thing full grown? or where was the awaking? (*The Everlasting Man* was helping me here.) There were really only two answers possible: either in Hinduism or in Christianity. Everything else was either a preparation for, or else (in the French sense) a *vulgarisation* of, these. Whatever you could find elsewhere you could find better in one of these. But Hinduism seemed to have two disqualifications. For one thing, it appeared to be not so much a moralised and philosophical maturity of Paganism as a mere oil-and-water coexistence of philosophy side by side with Paganism unpurged; the Brahmin meditating in the forest, and, in the village a few miles away, temple-prostitution, *sati*, cruelty, monstrosity. And secondly, there was no such historical claim as in Christianity. I was by now too experienced in literary criticism to regard the Gospels as myths. They had not the mythical taste. And yet the very matter which they set down in their artless, historical fashion—those narrow, unattractive Jews, too blind to the mythical wealth of the Pagan world around them—was precisely the matter of the great myths. If ever a myth had become fact, had been incarnated, it would be just like this. And nothing else in all literature was just like this. Myths were like it in one way. Histories were like it

in another. But nothing was simply like it. And no person was like the Person it depicted; as real, as recognisable, through all that depth of time, as Plato's Socrates or Boswell's Johnson (ten times more so than Eckermann's Goethe or Lockhart's Scott), yet also numinous, lit by a light from beyond the world, a god. But if a god—we are no longer polytheists—then not a god, but God. Here and here only in all time the myth must have become fact; the Word, flesh; God, Man. This is not "a religion", nor "a philosophy". It is the summing up and actuality of them all.³³³

The Five Deaths of the Faith

In the penultimate chapter of this book, Chesterton talks about the five deaths of the faith and how Christianity has risen from the dead every time. What were these five deaths? Chesterton answers, uncharacteristically, in one succinct sentence:

> At least five times, therefore, with the Arian and the Albigensian, with the Humanist skeptic, after Voltaire and after Darwin, the Faith has to all appearance gone to the dogs. In each of these five cases it was the dog that died.³³⁴

Since some of these movements and historical figures will not be well known to all readers, perhaps a few words of description are in order. Arianism has already been covered, briefly, above. According to The Catholic Encyclopedia, Albigensianism was:

> A neo-Manichæan sect that flourished in southern France in the twelfth and thirteenth centuries. The name Albigenses, given them by the Council of Tours (1163) prevailed towards the end of the twelfth century and was for a long time applied to all the heretics of the south of France. They were also called Catharists (*katharos*, pure), though in reality they were only a branch of the Catharistic movement. The rise and spread of the new doctrine in southern France was favoured by various circumstances, among which may be mentioned: the fascination exercised by the readily-grasped dualistic principle; the remnant of Jewish and Mohammedan doctrinal elements; the wealth, leisure, and imaginative mind of the inhabitants of Languedoc; their contempt for the Catholic clergy, caused by the ignorance and the worldly, too frequently scandalous, lives of the latter; the protection of an overwhelming majority of the nobility, and the intimate local blending of national aspirations and religious sentiment.³³⁵

Humanism began with the Renaissance in the sixteenth century and the revival of classical learning. However, Humanism came to emphasize the value of human thought over against faith in God, pitting rationalism against fideism. Voltaire was the pen name of François-Marie d'Arouet, who lived from 1694 to 1778. He was a French writer and public activist who played a defining role in the eighteenth-century Enlightenment. Then, of course, Charles Darwin (1809-1882) was the English naturalist and geologist known for his contributions to evolutionary theory.

No doubt, Chesterton could have picked other movements, events, and figures in church history to illustrate his point, and he does indeed allude to some others. Yet, the main point remains the same:

> Christendom has had a series of revolutions and in each one of them Christianity has died. Christianity has died many times and risen again; for it had a God who knew the way out of the grave.[336]

The only reason the Church has risen from the grave every time is because of the truth spoken by Jesus, "Heaven and earth shall pass away, but my words shall not pass away." (Matthew 24:35)

Conclusion

Chesterton concludes this book by reminding the reader that it has been a response to H. G. Wells' *Outline of History*. While Chesterton finds Wells' work admirable as an accumulation of history, he finds it false as an outline; the proportions are wrong. However, Chesterton also admits he may have failed in the same way, by getting the proportions of history wrong. He confesses that: "it would be far nearer the truth to tell the tale very simply, like a primitive myth about a man who made the sun and stars or a god who entered the body of a sacred monkey."[337] Therefore, that is what Chesterton proceeds to do in the rest of his conclusion: remind his readers of the main points of his book in the form of a story. Of course, this is what Lewis found most effective as well: to re-tell the story of Christianity in the form of a tale rather than as straight apologetic. Lewis did this in his Narnia tales, but also in his Cosmic Trilogy, in *Till We Have Faces*, in *Screwtape*, in *The Great Divorce*, in *The Pilgrim's Regress*, in fact, in all of his fiction.

Chesterton concludes his story by saying that if the faith it tells about "were an error, it seems as if the error could hardly have lasted a day."[338] Instead, it has lasted for two thousand years, "and nowhere in this sad world are boys happier in apple-trees, or men in more equal chorus singing as they tread the vine, than under the fixed flash of this instant and intolerant enlightenment."[339]

Appendices

In the two appendices at the end of the book, one "On Prehistoric Man" and the other "On Authority and Accuracy," Chesterton responds to certain criticisms that he expects the book to garner. Regarding prehistoric humanity, Chesterton realizes that some critics will ask: "What does Chesterton know about the matter?" Chesterton pleads:

> I am conscious that this attempt to express it in terms of innocence may exaggerate even my own ignorance. Without any pretence of scientific research or information, I should be sorry to have it thought that I knew no more than what was needed, in that passage, of the stages into which primitive humanity has been divided.[340]

Chesterton is aware that the story of prehistoric humanity is more elaborate than he has had time or space to comment upon. Nonetheless, he takes one final shot at the scientists:

> I am also aware of the story of the Cro-Magnon skull that was much larger and finer than a modern skull. It is a very funny story; because an eminent evolutionist, awakening to a somewhat belated caution, protested against anything being inferred from one specimen. It is the duty of a solitary skull to prove that our fathers were our inferiors. Any solitary skull presuming to prove that they were superior is felt to be suffering from swelled head.[341]

Yet, in the very first paragraph of the second appendix, Chesterton denies that he is scoffing at serious scientific work. Lewis too was accused of being anti-science. However, it would seem that Lewis was not as guilty of hitching his apologetic to any particular, scientific theory of his own time. Chesterton seems much more dated in this regard.[342] Furthermore, Lewis, by taking his stand with the theistic evolutionists (see *The Problem of Pain*) continues to reach a broader audience, in my opinion, than Chesterton who appears decidedly against the acceptance of any aspect of evolutionary theory.

Virgil

THE AENEID BY VIRGIL

Lewis' Reading of Virgil

The first recorded instance of C. S. Lewis reading Virgil took place sometime between 1911 and 1913, when he was in his early teens, as a pupil at Cherbourg House (a preparatory school in Great Malvern, England).[343] Lewis writes about this experience in *Surprised by Joy*....

> The ludicrous burden of false duties in prayer provided, of course, an unconscious motive for wishing to shuffle off the Christian faith; but about the same time, or a little later, conscious causes of doubt arose. One came from reading the classics. Here, especially in Virgil, one was presented with a mass of religious ideas; and all teachers and editors took it for granted from the outset that these religious ideas were sheer illusion. No one ever attempted to show in what sense Christianity fulfilled Paganism or Paganism prefigured Christianity. The accepted position seemed to be that religions were normally a mere farrago of nonsense, though our own, by a fortunate exception, was exactly true. The other religions were not even explained, in the earlier Christian fashion, as the work of devils. That I might, conceivably, have been brought to believe. But the impression I got was that religion in general, though utterly false, was a natural growth, a kind of endemic nonsense into which humanity tended to blunder. In the midst of a thousand such religions stood our own, the thousand and first, labeled True. But on what grounds could I believe in this exception? It obviously was in some general sense the same kind of thing as all the rest. Why was it so differently treated? Need I, at any rate, continue to treat it differently? I was very anxious not to.[344]

Virgil's influence upon Lewis' move to atheism was already accomplished before his studies under fellow atheist and tutor, William Kirkpatrick, began. However, once Lewis arrived at his tutor's home in Surrey, his study of Virgil,[345] and *The Aeneid* in particular, in Latin, began in earnest. By March 1915, he was asking his father to purchase *Aeneid* VII and VIII.[346] It is interesting to note that at this time Lewis found Homer to be better than Virgil.[347] However, in the long run, Virgil was to have the greater influence upon him. By the end of

1915, Lewis was becoming so familiar with Virgil that he quoted him from the Latin, in an offhand way, in a letter to his father.[348]

While he was in hospital in France, with trench fever, during the First World War, Lewis ordered "a couple of books of Vergil" in Latin from a bookseller in London.[349] He was soon wounded in the war and sent to London to recover at Endsleigh Palace Hospital. Once he was well enough, he enjoyed visiting various secondhand booksellers. In one shop, he was shown a priceless old copy of Virgil that he enjoyed seeing.[350] Lewis continued reading Virgil, among many other authors, immediately before his demobilization from the army.[351] When he finally went up to Oxford to begin his classics degree in earnest, at the beginning of 1919, he had to read all of Homer, Virgil, Demosthenes, and four Greek plays, as well as a special subject instead of verse. By February, he had already read halfway through the Iliad in Greek.[352]

Lewis' copy of the works of Virgil in Latin, which resides in the library of the University of North Carolina at Chapel Hill, indicates that Lewis finished reading the works for the first time on 20 September 1919.[353] Lewis' copy contains his underlining of particular words in the text with brief, often one-word, notations regarding translation in the margin. The volume also contains Lewis' single paragraph synopses of each Book of the *Aeneid*, as well as occasional footnotes in Lewis' hand. Lewis even created maps on the endpapers—one of Italy with particular sites noted, and another of the journey of Aeneas and the Trojans.

In the summer of 1920, Lewis was reading "Virgil through again".[354] In fact, Lewis became so familiar with the *Aeneid* that it became natural for him to use scenes from Virgil's great work as illustrations or analogies in his correspondence.[355]

In a letter to one of his university friends, Leo Baker, Lewis presents his characteristic view of originality, a perspective he learned from Virgil:

> This is one of the privileges of art, that all things are in common: imitation, if it is forgotten, matters not, and, if it lives, is justified and does not diminish the originality of the borrower. The notion of literary property was brought by philistines from the valley of the gorribeenmen into Helicon where it has no weight nor meaning. All poetry is one, and I love to see the great notes repeated. Homer and Virgil wrote lines not for their own works alone but for the use of all their followers. A plague on these moderns scrambling for what they call originality—like men trying to lift themselves off the earth by pulling at their own braces: as if by shutting their eyes to the work of the masters they were likely to create new things themselves.[356]

Like all of his favorite books, Lewis read the *Aeneid* many times.[357] In the spring of 1932, he mentions in a letter to his brother that he has been reading it again.³⁵⁸ In a letter to Dom Bede Griffiths in 1939, Lewis quotes a phrase from Aeneid VI 126: "facilis descensus Averno", "easy is the descent to the underworld".³⁵⁹ Screwtape makes a similar statement at the end of Letter XII: "Indeed the safest road to Hell is the gradual one—the gentle slope, soft underfoot, without sudden turnings, without milestones, without signposts."³⁶⁰

In a letter to Dorothy Sayers in 1946, Lewis mentions that he is reading the *Aeneid* yet again and he recounts to her what he is getting out of it:

> The effect is one of the immense *costliness* of a vocation combined with a complete conviction that it is worth it. The whole story is littered with the cost—Creusa, Dido, Anchises, Palinurus, Pallas, Lausus, Camilla. Did he do it so well because the making of the poem had for him the same costliness wh. the founding of Rome had for the characters? All the Alexandrian in him that wanted to write more *Bucolics*, all the countryman that wanted to write more *Georgics*, was sacrificed and long hung (like the Trojan women) *miserum inter amorem Praesentis terrae et fatis vocantia regna*.³⁶¹ i.e. the supreme instance of the poet who becomes far better than he was precisely by writing the poem wh. wasn't exactly what he thought he'd like to write.³⁶²

Lewis finished this particular re-reading of the *Aeneid* on Boxing Day and wrote to the poet Ruth Pitter, saying that he would like to discuss the poem at length with her during their next meeting.³⁶³

In one of his few letters to his friend and Oxford colleague, J. R. R. Tolkien, Lewis compares *The Lord of the Rings* to the *Aeneid*. He says that LOTR "will rank, along with the *Aeneid* as one of what I call my 'immediately sub-religious' books." Then Lewis continues:

> Indeed (unexpectedly) the general aroma seems to me more like the *Aeneid* than anything else, in spite of all your Northernness. This is partly because both (a.) Are so often sylvan (b.) Have *strategy*, as distinct from mere combat, (c.) Suggest an enormous past behind the action.³⁶⁴

On July 24, 1946, Lewis wrote once again to his friend, Ruth Pitter; in the midst of his letter, he reminded her, sadly, that no line of poetry is immortal. "A change in education can blot out a whole dead language and Virgil ceases to be."³⁶⁵ Lewis' point was certainly prophetic. Among the generation of students after Lewis' time, both in the United States and in the United Kingdom, Latin ceased to be a required subject. Thus, unlike Lewis and his generation, I, and many others, have grown up never reading Virgil in school.

In a letter to I. O. Evans, written on February 28, 1949, Lewis stated that: "art can teach (and much great art deliberately set out to do so) without ceasing to be art."³⁶⁶ Furthermore, Lewis believed that there are certain books where "the doctrine is as good on its own merits as the art." Among authors whose teaching is as good as their art, Lewis numbered Bunyan, Chesterton, Tolstoy, Charles Williams, and Virgil.[367]

Lewis often quoted Virgil in his letters[368] and in his diary[369] almost in the same manner as one might quote a phrase from the Bible. The *Aeneid* became part of the warp and woof of Lewis' mind. In fact, in one place in his diary, before his return to Christian faith, Lewis said he preferred the Virgilian view of heaven to the Christian one.[370] With his friends and colleagues as well as by himself, Lewis would sometimes play a sort of game by which he would pick out quotes from Virgil's works at random and read them, in an effort to predict the future, similar to the way that some people read the Bible.[371]

In a letter to Dom Bede Griffiths on April 23, 1951, Lewis wrote:

> The *Prelude* has accompanied me through all the stages of my pilgrimage: it and the *Aeneid* (which I never feel you value sufficiently) are the two long poems to wh. I most often return.[372]

In a letter to Herbert Palmer on January 25, 1954, Lewis made a negative reference to Cecil Day-Lewis' translation of the *Aeneid* published in 1952. "And the cunning devils are now translating Virgil & Sophocles into the modern style so as [to] make people believe that poetry *always was* the same sort of muck it is now."[373]

Given this comment, one might wonder what translation of the *Aeneid* Lewis preferred. He tells us in *English Literature in the Sixteenth Century*. It is Gavin Douglas' Scots version from 1513. Lewis writes,

> ... the real Virgil is very much less 'classical' than we had supposed. To read the Latin again with Douglas's version fresh in our minds is like seeing a favourite picture after it has been cleaned. Half the 'richness' and 'sobriety' which we have been taught to admire turns out to have been only dirt; the 'brown trees' disappear and where the sponge has passed the glowing reds, the purples, and the transparent blues leap into life.[374]

Lewis in fact attempted his own translation of the *Aeneid*, apart from his school assignments, apparently just for the fun of it. The first mention we have of this is in his diary entry for 11-14 August 1922. Lewis says that he sought to amuse a friend with his attempt to translate the opening of Book II of the *Aeneid* into French alexandrines.[375] By the time he published *The Pilgrim's Regress* in 1933, Lewis included his own translation of Book V, Lines 626-635, at the beginning of his own Book VII: Southward Along the Canyon.[376] That same year, Lewis wrote of his desire to translate the *Aeneid* into rhyming Alexandrines in a letter to Edmund Blunden.[377] By March of 1935, Lewis was able to report to his friend, Owen Barfield, that he had translated two hundred lines of the *Aeneid*.³⁷⁸ Lewis apparently continued working on his translation intermittently over the course of the next decade. He gave a snippet of his translation of *Aeneid* VII, 172, in *The Problem of Pain*, published in 1940.³⁷⁹ In a letter to his son Christopher on 22 September 1943, J. R. R. Tolkien referred to Lewis reading an extract of his translation to the Inklings.³⁸⁰ Tolkien mentioned another reading, again in a letter to his son a year later.³⁸¹ Lewis quoted his own translation of *Aeneid* I, 34, in his tribute to the work of his friend Charles Williams, entitled *Arthurian Torso*, published in 1948.³⁸² In a letter to Martin Kilmer on March 27, 1959, Lewis once again mentioned his desire to translate the *Aeneid* and quoted his own translation of *Aeneid* I, 32-33.³⁸³ Lewis' final reference to the *Aeneid* along with his translation of VI, 624, appeared in *The Discarded Image*, published posthumously in 1964.³⁸⁴ Thus, Lewis tinkered at his own translation of bits and pieces of the *Aeneid* virtually throughout his life.³⁸⁵ Thanks to A. T. Reyes, the extant portions of that translation work, including all of *Aeneid* I (758 lines) and substantial portions of Book II (516 lines) and Book VI (253 lines), have now been published.³⁸⁶

On at least one occasion, and probably more often, Lewis recommended to a student the *Aeneid* from the Loeb Library as one of the most relevant Latin books to have under one's belt in preparation for reading English at Oxford.³⁸⁷ He also referred to the Oxford Virgil in Latin, edited by Frederick Arthur Hirtzel, published in 1900.³⁸⁸ The latter was, most likely, one of the editions of the works of Virgil that Lewis most often used for his own reading.

The reader may wonder, given Lewis' deep and abiding interest in Virgil, and specifically in the *Aeneid*, whether he ever wrote a commentary on Virgil's great epic.³⁸⁹ As you may be aware, Lewis never wrote a full-length preface to the *Aeneid*. However, he did include a chapter on "Virgil and the Subject of Secondary Epic" in his *Preface to Paradise Lost*.³⁹⁰ Lewis' *Preface* is, of course, well worth reading in its entirety, and the chapter on Virgil has many worthwhile insights, too many to include here. However, I do wish to point out a few highlights. The chapter goes a long way toward explaining why the *Aeneid* was such an important book to Lewis. He begins the chapter by saying,

> The epic subject, as later critics came to understand it, is Virgil's invention; he has altered the very meaning of the word epic.³⁹¹

> How, you may well wonder, has Virgil done this? He has accomplished this great feat by taking a single national legend and treating "it in such a way that we feel the vaster theme to be somehow implicit in it.... If I am not mistaken it is almost the first poem which carries a real sense of the 'abysm of time'."³⁹²

One question I wondered about for some time was this: "Why did Lewis, in the end, choose Virgil as one of his most influential authors over Homer?"

Lewis' Top Ten

I believe the answer lies in what Lewis sees as the great theme of the *Aeneid*, namely Vocation. Regarding this Virgilian sense of Vocation Lewis says, "Nothing separates him so sharply from Homer, and that, sometimes, in places where they are superficially most alike."[393] For Aeneas, following the calling of the gods to find a new homeland for his people does not necessarily lead to happiness. However, once Aeneas has heard this call, he realizes there will be no happiness for him unless he follows it to the end.[394]

This idea of vocation was obviously quite important in Lewis' own life and thought. As a young man, he longed to become a great epic poet like Virgil. However, after the failure of his epic poem *Dymer*, Lewis essentially gave up on this dream. A few years later, he felt called of God to return to the Christian faith he had abandoned in his teens, and with that call came the vocation to write works of Christian fantasy and theology, a vocation that Lewis followed with the devotion of an Aeneas to the end of his life. In fact, Lewis compared himself to Aeneas in an unfinished autobiographical poem written shortly after his return to Christian faith in 1931.[395]

Given that the *Aeneid* was so important to Lewis, one might be tempted to think that Lewis would gladly draw up a list of literary masterpieces like it, that every educated person should read. However, such was not the case. Lewis was once asked to draw up just such a list of literary masterpieces, but he refused to comply with this request saying:

> I would rather see young men beginning from where they are and being led on from one thing to another: e.g. that Milton shd. lead them *either* to Virgil and Homer (and therefore to a really serious study of Latin or Greek) *or* to Dante (and therefore to a whole course of Medieval and Italian studies). That, after all, is how every educated person's development has actually come about.[396]

That is certainly how my development has come about, and I imagine yours as well. Reading Lewis has led me to read some other authors I never would have read had it not been for his introduction. Thus, on to Virgil we go . . . .

Virgil's Life[397]

Publius Vergilius Maro was born on 15 October in the year 70 BCE. According to Donatus,

> While he was in his mother's womb, she dreamt that she gave birth to a laurel-branch, which on touching the earth took root and grew at once to the size of a full-grown tree, covered with fruits and flowers of various kinds; and on the following day, when she was on the way to a neighbouring part of the country with her husband, she turned aside and gave birth to her child in a ditch beside the road. They say that the infant did not cry at its birth, and had such a gentle expression as even then to give assurance of an unusually happy destiny.[398]

Virgil was raised on a farm in the Andes district near Mantua in northern Italy. His parents were of humble origin; his father may have been a potter, although there is also a story that Virgil's father was at first the hired man of a certain Magus, and later became his son-in-law because of his diligence. Virgil's father greatly increased his property by buying up woodlands and raising bees. Not surprisingly, Virgil's *Georgics* deal with the life and habits of bees as a model for human society.

Virgil's father eventually became blind. The poet had two brothers: Silo, who died in childhood, and Flaccus, who lived longer, but whose death Virgil laments under the name of Daphnis in his *Eclogues*.[399]

Virgil wrote his first poem while still a boy. He composed the following couplet about a schoolmaster named Ballista, who was stoned to death because of his evil reputation for brigandage:

> Under this mountain of stones Ballista is covered and buried
> Wayfarer, now night and day follow your course without fear.

Apparently, over time, Virgil's father developed sufficient wealth to offer to his son the best education then available. Somewhere between the age of ten and twelve, Virgil's father sent his son to school in Cremona, the winter headquarters of Caesar's army. Virgil was probably there when Julius Caesar published *The Gallic Wars*. Among other studies, he gave attention also to medicine and to mathematics.[400] After receiving the "toga virilis,"[401] Virgil continued his education briefly at Milan before venturing to Rome for the study of rhetoric.

When he was sixteen years old, Virgil wrote a poem entitled *Culex*. Donatus explains the story behind the poem....

> When a shepherd exhausted by the heat, had fallen asleep under a tree,

and a snake was creeping upon him, a gnat flew from a marsh and stung the shepherd between his two temples; he at once crushed the gnat and killed the snake; then he made a tomb for the insect, inscribed with this couplet:

> "Thee, tiny gnat, well deserving, the flock's grateful keeper now offers
> For the gift of his life due funeral rites in requital."[402]

Virgil followed the traditional course of preparation for a life in politics. He joined the school of Epidius where Octavian and Marc Antony were also students. However, Virgil did not enjoy rhetoric; thus, after arguing one case before the law courts,[403] he abandoned the life of a lawyer to pursue the study of philosophy.

Donatus informs us of the following details of Virgil's personal life:

> He was tall and of full habit, with a dark complexion and a rustic appearance. His health was variable; for he very often suffered from stomach and throat troubles, as well as with headache; and he also had frequent hemorrhages. He ate and drank but little. He was especially given to passions for boys, and his special favorites were Cebes and Alexander, whom he calls Alexis in the second poem of his "Bucolics." This boy was given him by Asinius Pollio, and both his favorites had some education, while Cebes was even a poet.[404]

Virgil departed from Rome and settled in Naples where he joined "the Garden," a school of philosophy run by Siron the Epicurean. Virgil remained under Siron's tutelage until Siron's death at which time he possibly inherited Siron's villa. Philosophy was not the only subject of discussion in "the Garden." Siron's pupils also studied poetry. They read Catullus and Lucretius as well as writing their own verse following the Alexandrian style. Virgil probably wrote a number of his minor poems at this time. Of this period in Virgil's life, tradition claims…

> … at Naples he was commonly called "Parthenias," [* "The Maiden"] and that whenever he appeared in public in Rome, where he very rarely went, he would take refuge in the nearest house, to avoid those who followed and pointed him out.[405]

Does Virgil's nickname, "The Maiden," also suggest that he was effeminate in character? No one knows for certain, though this is a possible interpretation of the tradition.

We know little of Virgil's activities during the Civil War (49-45 BCE). We do know that when Octavius came to power and took the title Caesar Augustus, he offered Virgil the property of a man who had gone into exile. However, Virgil could not make up his mind to accept it. Donatus claims that Virgil "possessed nearly ten million sesterces from the generous gifts of friends, and he had a house at Rome on the Esquiline, near the gardens of Maecenas, although he usually lived in retirement in Campania and in Sicily." In Rome, Virgil met Horace, Varius (the epic poet), and many other men of letters. There, he became the leader of a group under the patronage of Octavius and Maecenas; the group functioned as a type of semi-official committee on literature for promoting the peace and welfare of the Roman Empire.[406]

Virgil composed his pastoral poetry known as the *Eclogues* (also called the *Bucolics*) sometime between 42 and 39 BCE.[407] James Rhoades notes that, "In the *Eclogues* there is already a hint that Virgil was thinking of writing an epic: 'When I tried to make a poem of warring kings, Apollo twitched my ear....'"[408]

According to tradition, Virgil wrote the *Eclogues*...

> ... especially for the purpose of singing the praises of Asinius Pollio, Alfenus Varus, and Cornelius Gallus, because at the time of the assignment of the lands beyond the Po, which were divided among the veterans by order of the triumvirs after the victory at Philippi, these men had saved him from ruin.... The success of the "Bucolics" on their first appearance was such that they were even frequently rendered by singers on the stage. [409]

The publication of the *Eclogues* immediately established Virgil as the most celebrated poet of his day. Tacitus (50-117 CE) later said that on one occasion when the *Eclogues* were read aloud in a theater and Virgil was present, the audience stood and acclaimed the poet just as they would have done for the emperor.[410]

After the *Eclogues*, Virgil wrote the *Georgics*, between 38 and 29 BCE. In these poems, Virgil speaks of the temple he will build with Caesar "in the middle," and he asserts that he will bring to Caesar lasting fame. This would not be accomplished until Virgil wrote his final epic poem, the *Aeneid*.[411] When writing the *Georgics*, Virgil composed orally, as many as twenty lines every morning. A slave would read these lines back to Virgil in the afternoon at which time the poet would reduce and edit them "like a she bear licking her cubs into shape".[412] The *Georgics* are didactic poems offering advice to farmers about human beings and the environment.[413] Donatus claims that Virgil wrote these poems...

> ... in honour of Maecenas, because he had rendered him aid, when the poet was still but little known, against the violence of one of the veterans, from whom Vergil narrowly escaped death in a quarrel about his farm.[414]

Furthermore, Donatus relates that when Augustus returned after his victory at Actium (31 BCE), he lingered at Atella to treat his throat. During this time, Virgil read the *Georgics* to Augustus for four days straight. A man named Alaecenas took his turn reading whenever Virgil's voice failed. According to Donatus, Virgil's own delivery, however, was "sweet and wonderfully effective". In fact, the Roman stoic philosopher Seneca (4 BCE- 65 CE) later quoted the poet Julius Montanus as declaring that he would have stolen some of Virgil's work, if he could also have stolen his voice, expression, and dramatic power. Apparently, the same verses that sounded quite fine when Virgil read them, fell flat on the lips of another.[415]

Virgil composed the *Aeneid* during the last ten years of his life, from 29 to 19 BCE, possibly at the invitation of Augustus, as a mythic account of the origin of Rome. Ever since the writing of his early poems, Virgil had pondered the preeminence of the Julian line of Roman rulers.[416] Thus, the *Aeneid* includes oblique praise of the emperor and in some ways functions as an Octavian panegyric.[417] The *Aeneid* mirrors both of Homer's epic poems, the first six books patterned after the *Odyssey* and the last six books after the *Iliad*. Donatus informs us more deeply about the poet's supposed method of composition in the case of the *Aeneid*....

> ...after writing a first draft in prose and dividing it into twelve books he proceeded to turn into verse one part after another, taking them up just as he fancied, in no particular order. And that he might not check the flow of his thought, he left some things unfinished, and, so to speak, bolstered others up with very slight words, which, as he jocosely used to say, were put in like props, to support the structure until the solid columns should arrive.[418]

Tradition claims that when Augustus was away on his Cantabrian campaign (29-19 BCE) he demanded that Virgil send him something from the *Aeneid*, either the first draft of the poem or any section of it that he pleased. Virgil responded:

> Regarding my *Aeneas*, if I had anything worth your hearing, I would gladly send it, but the thing is so inchoate that it almost seems to me that I must have been out of my mind to have started such a work.[419]

It would be another two or three years before Virgil would eventually read to Augustus three books of the *Aeneid*: the second, fourth, and sixth. According to Donatus,

> The last of these produced a remarkable effect on Octavia [the wife of the emperor], who was present at the reading; for it is said that when he reached the verses about her son, "Thou shalt be Marcellus," she

fainted and was with difficulty revived. He [Virgil] gave readings also to various others, but never before a large company, selecting for the most part passages about which he was in doubt, in order to get the benefit of criticism.[420]

In the last year of his life, Virgil decided he wanted to give the final touches to the *Aeneid*. Thus, he determined that he would travel to Greece and Asia to devote three years to improving his epic work. Then, when he was finished, his plan was to give the rest of his life to philosophy. Virgil met Augustus at Athens while the emperor was on his way home from the Orient. He decided that he would stay with the emperor and return to Rome with him. However, while visiting the neighboring town of Megara, after sitting in the hot sun, Virgil was taken with a fever. He made his health worse by continuing on his journey rather than resting. When he arrived at Brundisium (Brindisi), he was gravely ill and died there on September 21. Virgil's ashes were taken to Naples and placed in a tomb for which he himself composed his own epitaph:

> Mantua gave me birth, Calabria took me away, and now Naples holds me;
> I sang of pastures, farms, leaders.[421]

Immediately before his death, Virgil was still not satisfied with the state of the *Aeneid*. Unable to complete his planned revisions, Virgil called for his manuscript more than once that he might burn it. However, no one would bring him the manuscript of the *Aeneid* for this purpose. Virgil left his writings jointly to his friends Varius and Tucca, with the stipulation that they should publish nothing that he himself would not have given to the world. However, Varius published the *Aeneid* at Augustus' request, making only a few slight corrections, and even leaving the incomplete lines just as they were.[422]

The *Aeneid* quickly received great acclaim. The poet Sextus Propertius (50-15 BCE) did not hesitate to declare upon hearing the *Aeneid*:

> Yield, ye Roman writers; yield, ye Greeks;
> A greater than the Iliad is born.[423]

What was Virgil's legacy? For one thing, the *Aeneid* became a school text almost immediately upon Virgil's death, and remained a key school text for young people learning Latin, down to the twentieth century.[424] Secondly, and most importantly for Christians, Virgil:

> Became for later generations a harbinger of Christianity, a prophet who had foretold the birth of Christ in an eclogue, and Dante's guide to the gates of Paradise in *The Divine Comedy*.[425]

In *Reflections on the Psalms*, Lewis commented on the seeming prophecy of the birth of Christ from the pen of the great poet....

Lewis' Top Ten

Virgil, writing not very long before the birth of Christ, begins a poem thus: "The great procession of the ages begins anew. Now the Virgin returns, the reign of Saturn returns, and the new child is sent down from high heaven." It goes on to describe the paradisal age which this nativity will usher in. And of course throughout the Middle Ages it was taken that some dim prophetic knowledge of the birth of Christ had reached Virgil, probably through the Sibylline Books. He ranked as a Pagan prophet. Modern scholars would, I suppose, laugh at the idea. They might differ as to what noble or imperial couple were being thus extravagantly complimented by a court poet on the birth of a son; but the resemblance to the birth of Christ would be regarded, once more, as an accident.... If this is luck, it is extraordinary luck.... What Virgil would have said, if he had learned the truth, I do not know. (Or may we more charitably speak, not of what Plato and Virgil and the mythmakers "would have said" but of what they said? For we can pray with good hope that they now know and have long since welcomed the truth; "many shall come from the east and the west and sit down in the kingdom.")[426]

The Aeneid: A Synopsis[427]

Book I: A Fateful Haven

Virgil begins the *Aeneid* by announcing his theme. He is going to be telling the story of how Aeneas made his way from Troy to Italy and founded the precursor to Rome. Virgil also reveals that Aeneas is going to have a very difficult time. This is because the goddess Juno is angry with him. Juno is mad at Aeneas for two reasons. First, she does not like Aeneas because he is a Trojan. Juno hates the Trojans because Paris, a Trojan prince, once picked Venus over her and Minerva in a beauty contest. This made Juno and Minerva take the Greek side during the Trojan War.

Second, Juno hates Aeneas because she loves Carthage. Juno knows that, in the future, Rome and Carthage are destined to fight a series of three major wars. These battles, known as the Punic Wars, will result in the complete destruction of Carthage. Thus, since Aeneas is on his way to found Rome, Juno is against him.

Juno first catches sight of Aeneas and his fleet as they are sailing past Sicily. She does not like this, and decides to make things difficult for Aeneas, whether the Fates like it or not. The first thing she does is to find Aeolus, the king of the winds. Juno tells Aeolus to stir up the sea against the Trojans; she says she will give him one of her nymphs to marry, in return for his help. Aeolus agrees to this plan. He takes his spear and pounds on the mountain where the winds are locked up. Out come the East Wind and the South Wind. They speed down to where the Trojans are sailing and stir up a storm against them. As the storm starts to pick up, Aeneas exclaims how he wishes he had died back home in Troy. Three ships crash and three are stuck on sandbars. Just then, Neptune hears the commotion going on above him. He pokes his eyes out of the water, and is not pleased with what he sees. Neptune immediately reprimands the winds for stirring up the ocean without his permission. Before he is finished speaking, the storm ends.

Aeneas and his remaining ships decide to head for the nearest land, which happens to be Libya. Once they have pulled into a convenient natural harbor, Aeneas and his men disembark. They make a fire and eat grain by the seashore.

While his men are eating, Aeneas and his comrade Achates climb a nearby hill to scan the sea for any sign of their lost ships. They do not see them. Instead, they find a herd of wild deer. Aeneas chases after them and shoots seven—one for each of his ships. Then he takes the deer down to the shore, and gives his men a speech, reminding them of how much they have suffered already. He tells them that one day they may even look back nostalgically on these hardships. (This is one of Lewis' favorite quotes from *The Aeneid*.) Aeneas is putting on a brave face for his men—inside, he feels more grief for their lost companions than anyone else. Still, the Trojans feast on the deer and regain their strength.

That evening, Jupiter, the king of the gods, is looking down at the world. Just then, Venus appears, the goddess of love, who also happens to be Aeneas' mother. Venus complains to Jupiter about how Aeneas and his men have to suffer so much, when other Trojans, like Antenor, have already been able to settle in various parts of Italy.

Jupiter says that he is going to allow Aeneas to make it to Italy. He then explains how Aeneas, when he gets to Italy, is going to have to fight a war against the local tribe of the Rutulians. After that, he will reign for only three years, but then his son, Ascanius, will rule for another thirty years in the new capital of Alba Longa. This city will be the headquarters of the Trojans in Italy for three centuries, until the queen and priestess Ilia is impregnated by Mars, the god of war, and gives birth to Romulus and Remus. Romulus will found Rome. Jupiter says he will give the Romans unlimited power. This power will reach its peak during the time of Augustus, whose reign will bring about a great era of peace. After explaining all this, Jupiter sends down the god Hermes to prepare the Carthaginians to welcome Aeneas and the other Trojans.

That night, Aeneas lies awake, deep in thought. He decides to go exploring the next day with his friend Achates. While they are walking in the woods, Aeneas and Achates encounter Venus, who is disguised as a young huntress. Aeneas senses that something is not quite right. Thus, he asks the huntress what goddess she is. Venus maintains her disguise, saying that she is just an ordinary girl from that area.

Venus then informs Aeneas of some local history. She explains how Dido, the local queen, was once married to Sychaeus, the richest man of the city of Tyre. Her brother, Pygmalion, was the king of Tyre. Unfortunately, Pygmalion was very greedy, and ended up killing Sychaeus for his money. Pygmalion managed to keep this murder hidden from Dido for a little while, but then Sychaeus appeared to her in a dream and explained what had happened. Sychaeus told Dido to flee the city immediately; he also told her where some treasure was buried, to finance her trip. Dido gathered up some other men from Tyre and sailed over to North Africa, where they are now, and where she is building the city of Carthage.

Having completed her story, Venus asks Aeneas who he is. Aeneas replies by telling his name and his quest. He explains how he and his men have endured a great storm and have lost some of their companions.

Venus tells Aeneas that everything will be fine. She shows Aeneas where twelve swans are flapping around in peace, even though a little while ago an eagle was chasing them. Venus interprets this as a sign that Aeneas' compatriots are safe.

As Venus turns to leave, Aeneas recognizes her as his mother and asks about her disguise. Venus does not answer. Instead, she wraps Aeneas and Achates in a cloud of mist, making them invisible. This allows them to walk into the heart of Carthage. All around them, people are busy building the new city. Aeneas is jealous because the Carthaginians have a city and he does not. In the middle of the city, the people are building a temple to Juno. Aeneas goes up to the temple. On its gates, he sees depicted various scenes from the Trojan War. (Most of these are from Homer's *Iliad*.) Then, Queen Dido comes in with a group of attendants. She takes her seat in front of Juno's shrine.

At this point, representatives from all of the ships that Aeneas thought he had lost arrive safely, just as Venus predicted. The Trojans explain to Dido who they are and where they are going. They complain about the rough treatment they have received from the local people, and say that the gods are on their side. They ask for permission to stay in the area long enough to repair their ships; then they will either sail for Latium as planned (if they reconnect with Aeneas), or head to Sicily instead, where another Trojan, Acestes, has set himself up as king.

In response, Dido apologizes for any trouble they have encountered; she explains that she has had to increase security while her city is established. Then she tells them that she has heard of Aeneas. She says that the Trojans can go wherever they want, with a Carthaginian escort, or, if they wish, they may stay in Carthage as equal citizens. She says that she wishes Aeneas were present. Furthermore, she promises to send out scouts to search the coastline for him.

At that moment, the cloud vanishes from Achates and Aeneas. At the same time, Venus makes Aeneas look very impressive and handsome. Aeneas thanks Dido for her hospitality. Dido is impressed with Aeneas and tells him so, explaining how she also is an exile, from Tyre. She leads Aeneas into her palace and declares it a feast day.

Aeneas thinks about his son Ascanius and sends Achates back to the camp to bring him to the feast. He also tells him to bring some gifts for Dido. (Specifically, he asks him to bring some of the things that Helen brought with her to Troy.)

Venus decides to make Amor, the god of love, take Ascanius' form so he can infect Dido with love. Venus tells Amor that she will hide the real Ascanius away in one of her shrines so that no one will be the wiser. When Amor (in the guise of Ascanius) arrives with the gifts, he first goes up to Aeneas and greets him as his father. Then he goes and sits on Dido's lap. Amor inflames Dido with love for Aeneas, and slowly takes away her memory of her dead husband, Sychaeus.

At the end of the feast, Dido fills a huge bowl with wine, drinks from it, and starts passing it around. At the same time, the poet Iopas sings a song about the cosmos. Dido, who is growing more enthralled by the minute, asks Aeneas question after question about the Trojan War. Finally, she asks him how Troy was captured, and how he came to North Africa.

Book II: How They Took the City

After some initial hesitation, Aeneas begins to tell the story of Troy's downfall. Everything that follows in this book and the next is told by Aeneas, and so reflects his perspective. Aeneas begins by telling how the Greeks, unable to defeat the Trojans in battle, sail away from Troy. On the beach, they leave behind a giant wooden horse, with Greek warriors hidden inside it, though the Trojans do not know that yet. Something else the Trojans do not know is that the Greeks did not actually sail home. Instead, they made their way to the nearby island of Tenedos, and left their navy on the other side of the island.

The Trojans are amazed at the horse and come out of their city to have a better look at it. Some argue in favor of taking the horse inside the city. Others argue for destruction of the horse. Laocoön, a priest, comes down from the city to have a look. He urges the Trojans to beware of Greeks bearing gifts. He even guesses that there are Greeks hiding inside the horse, and he throws his spear at it. The wooden horse echoes, revealing that it is hollow.

The Trojans plan to follow Laocoön's advice and destroy the horse, but they are interrupted by a commotion coming from some shepherds, who step forward with a prisoner who is a Greek. The captive's name is Sinon, and he has a story to tell.

Sinon claims to be related to Palamedes, a Greek hero who opposed the Trojan War. Palamedes was executed on a trumped-up charge because of Ulysses' (Odysseus') trickery. Sinon says that because he complained about this injustice, Ulysses had it in for him. He also says that the Greeks tried several times to sail home, but every time they were held back by bad weather. He says that their problems only got worse after the construction of the wooden horse. Finally, the Greeks sent a man called Eurypylus to ask the oracle of Apollo what they should do. The oracle tells Eurypylus that a human sacrifice is required in order for them to get home, just as a human sacrifice was required for them to get to Troy. (On the way to Troy, the Greek king Agamemnon had to sacrifice his daughter, Iphigeneia, to convince the winds to blow the right way.) This makes the Greeks very nervous. Ulysses asks Calchas the soothsayer to interpret the true will of the gods. Calchas keeps silent for ten days, but finally gives into Ulysses' pestering, and names Sinon as the victim.

When the day of the sacrifice arrives, however, Sinon manages to escape. In the end, the Greeks sail off without finding him. Thus ends Sinon's first story. In conclusion, he begs the Trojans, in the name of the gods, to spare his life.

The Trojans feel pity for Sinon, and Priam orders them to remove his chains. At this point, Priam thinks it is high time to ask Sinon about the wooden horse on the beach. Sinon swears that he is no longer loyal to the Greeks. Then he explains how the Greeks' troubles began when Ulysses and Diomedes stole a statue of Minerva from the Trojan citadel. After they brought the statuette back to camp, however, strange things began to happen. The statuette started sweating, flaming, and moving its eyes, and the goddess herself kept appearing out of the ground amid flashes of lightning. Calchas, the seer, interpreted these events to mean that Troy could not be captured. They would have to sail home and wait for another sign from the gods before making war on Troy again. According to Sinon, it was on Calchas' orders that they constructed the horse, as a replacement for the statue of Minerva they had stolen. He says that the reason they made it so big was so that the Trojans would not be able to take it inside their city. Sinon tells the Trojans that if any of them damage the horse, it will bring destruction on all of Troy. On the other hand, if they take it inside the city, it will bring destruction on all the Greeks. Here ends Sinon's second story.

At this point, Laocoön, the priest who threw the spear at the side of the horse, starts making a sacrifice to Neptune, the god of the sea. Suddenly, two giant serpents slither out of the sea, crawl up to Laocoön, and strangle him and his two sons. Then the serpents make their way into Troy, to Minerva's citadel, and curl up behind the statue's shield. The Trojans interpret this as punishment from the gods for spearing the horse. They decide to take the horse inside the city. They actually have to knock a hole in the wall to bring it in.

Four times the horse is jarred on its way into the city, and four times the weapons of the Greeks inside clatter. However, the Trojans do not notice. Nonetheless, the Trojan princess Cassandra, who has the gift of prophecy, tries to prevent her people from taking the horse inside the city. Unfortunately, the gods have cursed her so that her predictions will not be believed.

Night falls. The Greek fleet returns to Troy from Tenedos. Sinon lets the Greeks out of the horse. They kill the Trojan sentries and open the city gates for their friends who are just arriving at the city.

Meanwhile, in the city, Aeneas is asleep. The Trojan warrior Hector appears to him in his dream, all covered in blood and dirt as he was on the day he was killed by the Greek hero Achilles. Hector tells Aeneas that Troy is about to be captured. Hector urges Aeneas to gather up his household gods and leave to establish a new city for his people elsewhere. Aeneas wakes up and climbs up to his roof. From there, he hears a terrible clamor, and can see numerous houses burning. His first thought is to arm himself for battle. Then, at his door appears Pantheus, the priest of Apollo, who is carrying some images of the gods, and leading his grandson. Aeneas asks Pantheus where they should take their stand to defend Troy, but Pantheus tells him that saving the city is hopeless. Nonetheless, Aeneas gathers up some companions and rushes into the fight. Together, they engage in battle with reckless courage. They kill some Greeks and take their equipment. With these disguises, they are able to join the ranks of other Greeks and kill them through subterfuge.

However, Coroebus, one of Aeneas' comrades, who also happens to be the husband of Cassandra, sees his wife being dragged out of Minerva's temple by some Greek warriors. Like a mad man, he rushes into the fight, and everyone else follows. In the chaos, they are struck by a series of missiles thrown by Trojans hiding out atop the temple; they mistake Aeneas and his comrades for Greeks because of their stolen armor.

Realizing the deception of Aeneas and company, the Greeks rally, and a furious battle breaks out in front of the temple. Many Trojans are killed, including Coroebus. The Trojans are distracted when they realize that Priam's palace is being besieged. Aeneas and some other men sneak in a back entrance to help. They make their way to the roof, where they knock a tower off onto the Greeks below. However, there are too many Greeks to fight off forever. The most fearsome of the Greeks is Neoptolemus, the son of Achilles.

Meanwhile, Priam puts on his armor and prepares to face down the Greeks, old and decrepit as he is. When his wife Hecuba sees him, however, she tells him to stop being such a fool. She makes him join her and some women who are clinging to an altar for safety. (They are assuming that the Greeks will not violate the holiness of the place.)

Just then, Polites, one of Priam's sons, rushes in, wounded, with Neoptolemus in pursuit. Neoptolemus catches up to him and kills him. Enraged, Priam prepares to attack Neoptolemus. Priam reminds Neoptolemus about how his father, Achilles, once had pity on him when he gave Hector's body back for burial. (This scene is described in Book 23 of Homer's *Iliad*.) Priam tells Neoptolemus that his horrible behavior makes it seem as if he is not a true son of Achilles. Priam feebly attacks his younger foe and does not even succeed in wounding him. Neoptolemus drags Priam through the blood of his son to the altar, and kills him there.

Aeneas, who has been watching this whole scene, is reminded of his own father, Anchises. On his way home, he meets Helen. She is trying to hide, afraid of both the Trojans and the Greeks. Aeneas is about to kill her, when his mother, Venus, appears and tells him not to blame her for the war. She says that what is happening to Troy is not Helen's fault; it is the will of the gods.

Venus takes the mist away from Aeneas' sight so he can see various gods at work destroying the city. Then Aeneas runs home, finds his father, and tells him to get ready to leave the city. However, Anchises refuses. He says that he has lived and suffered long enough. Creusa, Aeneas' wife, and Ascanius, his son, try to convince Anchises, but he is resistant.

Finally, Aeneas gathers his weapons in order to go out and die fighting. Creusa tells him to take her and Ascanius along with him. Just then, flames burst out of Ascanius' head, but do not burn him. Anchises prays for a sign from the gods, and suddenly a shooting star flashes overhead. Anchises accepts the sign and decides to go with Aeneas.

Now thinking of survival instead of suicide, Aeneas takes his father on his shoulders. He gives his father the household gods to carry. Then he takes Ascanius by the hand. After Aeneas tells some servants that they will meet up at a certain cypress tree by an inland gate of the city, they head off, with Creusa following behind. In a moment of confusion, however, Aeneas turns down some alleyways, and Creusa becomes lost. Aeneas does not realize this until they arrive at the cypress tree. He goes back alone through the flaming city, looking for his wife, but does not find her. Suddenly, her ghost appears and tells him that it is too late. She tells him to go to where the Tiber River flows. There he will receive a new kingdom and a new wife. Aeneas accepts Creusa's words and returns to the cypress tree, where many refugees have now gathered. Together, they set out on their voyage.

Book III: Sea Wanderings and Strange Meetings

Aeneas and his followers take refuge beneath Mount Ida, in the neighborhood of Troy. Here they set to work building a fleet. When summer arrives, they set sail. First, they head for Thrace, a region once allied with Troy. Aeneas plots out a settlement on the coast. Then he prepares to make a sacrifice. However, when he tries to pick some myrtle saplings to make a shelter for the altar, something strange happens: blood spurts out from the roots of the tree. Aeneas tries again, and more blood appears. Upset, Aeneas prays to the gods. Then he tries a third time. This time, a voice speaks from the ground, identifying himself as Polydorus, a Trojan. He explains that some men killed him with spears that then took root and turned into myrtle trees.

King Priam of Troy had sent Polydorus to Thrace with a shipment of gold. He was to give the gold to the king of Thrace for safekeeping while the Trojan War continued. Unfortunately, the Thracian king decided to take the gold for himself, which is why he had Polydorus killed.

After a brief consultation, Aeneas and the other leaders decide that this is not the best place to start a new city. Before setting sail, they hold funeral rites for Polydorus. Then, they sail to the island of Delos, where there is an oracle of the god Apollo. The oracle tells them to go to the original home of the Trojan people. There they will establish an empire that will rule the shores of the world for generations to come.

Aeneas' father, Anchises, knows where this original home is located. He explains that many years ago a man named Teucrus came from Crete. He sailed from there to Asia Minor, where he founded Troy. Therefore, Anchises recommends sailing for Crete.

The Trojans follow Anchises' advice and establish a city on the island of Crete. They are only there for a little while when a plague strikes them and their crops, and the sun dries up all the water. Anchises tells Aeneas that he should go back to Delos and ask the oracle for an explanation.

That night, while Aeneas is sleeping, the household gods begin speaking to him. They tell him to go to Italy, where another ancestor of the Trojans (Dardanus, Teucrus' son-in-law) came from. The next day, Aeneas relates this prophecy to Anchises, who agrees that they should go to Italy. Along the way, the fleet is battered by three days of storms. However, they eventually succeed in making their way to an island. What they do not know is that the Harpies (flying birdlike creatures with female faces) inhabit the island. All that the Trojans see is livestock roaming the shore unattended. When they go ashore to kill some of the animals for food, the Harpies swoop down and defile the meat. The Trojans try to fight them, but the Harpies fly away.

Then Celaeno, Queen of the Harpies, tells the Trojans that they will arrive in Italy safely, but they will be punished with hunger for what they did to the livestock. After praying to avert this calamity, the men set sail again, and eventually make it to the Leucas region of western Greece. They remain there for the winter, and then set sail again.

Next, they come to Chaonia in Epirus, a region of Northwestern Greece. In this place, they learn that Helenus, a son of the Trojan King Priam, has ended up ruling over some Greek cities. They also learn that he has married Andromache, who used to be the wife of the Trojan hero Hector, who is now dead. On their way to find their fellow Trojans, they meet Andromache herself, who is offering a sacrifice at a shrine she has made to her dead husband Hector.

Andromache faints when she sees Aeneas and his crew. However, when she wakes up she has a story to tell. After the fall of Troy, Achilles' son Neoptolemus enslaved her. However, he soon got tired of her and took a Spartan woman, Hermione, for his wife. Neoptolemus gave Andromache in marriage to her fellow captive, the Trojan Helenus.

Then Agamemnon's son, Orestes, who was in love with Hermione, killed Neoptolemus. Helenus inherited some land as a result, which is why he and Andromache have become the king and the queen in this part of Epirus.

Then Helenus arrives and leads Aeneas and company to his city, which turns out to be a miniature replica of Troy. After they stay there for a few days, Aeneas asks Helenus, who has the gift of prophecy, to tell them what is in store for them. Helenus offers sacrifices, and then a prophecy. He gives the Trojans a list of things for which they should watch out. He also tells them that, when they see a giant white pig suckling thirty white piglets, they will know that they have found their new homeland. Helenus tells the Trojans to stay away from Scylla and Charybdis, the narrows between Sicily and the mainland of Italy. Finally, he tells them to keep praying to Juno and once they arrive in Italy, they should go to the town of Cumae. There, they should consult with the Sibyl, a priestess and oracle. After this, Helenus gives the Trojans presents, with some special gifts for Anchises. Andromache also gives them gifts, with some special things for Ascanius, who reminds her of her dead son.

The Trojans set sail again. First, they go to Ceraunia, further up the coast of Greece. Then, on the east coast of Italy, they make a brief stop, before sailing again. They follow the coast of Italy south, and round the boot. Soon afterward, they feel the sea getting choppy. Anchises realizes that they are close to Scylla and Charybdis. He tells them to head away from it. They get away safely but are headed to the island of the Cyclopes, better known as Sicily. The volcanic Mt. Aetna is rumbling nearby. The Trojans make camp and spend the night in the forest.

In the morning, an emaciated man comes up to them out of the mist. (This character is like the Lord Rhoop whom the crew of *The Dawn Treader* meet on The Dark Island in Lewis' Narnia story.) It turns out that this man is a Greek named Achaemenides. Even though he is scared at first to fall in with a group of Trojans, he suddenly comes forward and throws himself at their mercy. He tells them that if they kill him, it will be better than what he would have suffered otherwise.

Achaemenides was a sailor from the fleet of Ulysses (Odysseus), who was left behind. He narrowly escaped from the Cyclops and has been hiding out in the forest for the past three months. (Book IX of Homer's *Odyssey* relates the story of Ulysses'/Odysseus' encounter with the Cyclops.) Achaemenides urges the Trojans to sail away as quickly as they can. At this point, Polyphemus, the Cyclops that Ulysses/Odysseus blinded, appears on the scene. Aeneas and his crew get away just in time, taking Achaemenides with them.

The Trojans continue sailing around the south coast of Sicily. When they stop at the city of Drepanum, tragedy strikes again: Aeneas' father, Anchises, dies. After this, Aeneas and his men make their way to Carthage.

Book IV: The Passion of the Queen

After Aeneas finishes his story, the next morning, Dido confides in her sister, Anna, that though she swore she would never love anyone after her dead husband, Sychaeus, she has fallen in love with Aeneas. However, Dido also decides she should not act on her feelings.

Anna questions whether the dead care about our faithfulness or not. More importantly, Carthage is surrounded by enemies, and a marriage between Dido and Aeneas would make for a strong and helpful military alliance.

The days pass, and Dido falls more deeply in love with Aeneas. Carthage's building projects stall with no oversight. The goddess Juno, seeing what is going on, recognizes Venus' handiwork. Juno discusses the situation with Venus, and suggests they lead Dido and Aeneas into marriage. Venus, who knows that Juno is against the Trojans, suggests seeking advice from Jupiter. Instead, Juno hatches a matchmaking plot. Dido and Aeneas go out hunting. Meanwhile, Juno sends rain, forcing Aeneas and Dido to take shelter in a cave. The two make love. As a result, Dido begins to see herself and Aeneas as married.

Rumor, a strange winged goddess with as many eyes and tongues as feathers, spreads the story of Juno's matchmaking efforts. King Iarbas, whose father is Jupiter, and who was once rejected by Dido, hears the story and complains to his father about it. Hearing his son's complaint, Jupiter dispatches the god Mercury to go and remind Aeneas that he is supposed to be establishing a city in Italy for the Trojans.

Mercury finds Aeneas supervising the construction of Carthage's walls and passes along Jupiter's message. Mercury encourages Aeneas to think about his son Ascanius, and what sort of legacy he is going to leave him. In response, Aeneas tells his people to prepare their fleet for departure. Aeneas tries to keep these preparations secret, but Dido hears of it and is furious. When she confronts Aeneas about it, he admits he is leaving. However, he points out that they are not, in fact, married and that he is a man on a mission who must establish a city for his people in Italy. It is the desire and plan of the gods; therefore, it is not his fault that he must leave.

Dido does not take this too well. She responds in anger to Aeneas; then, she runs away and faints. Dido's maids carry her back to her bedroom. The Trojans continue to prepare the fleet to set sail. When Dido awakes, she sees what is happening, and instructs her sister Anna to go and tell the Trojans to wait for better winds. Anna delivers the message, but Aeneas is unmoved.

Strange happenings trouble Dido: water blackens on her altars, and wine turns to blood. Voices speak from the shrine of her dead husband. Thus, Dido decides to commit suicide. She tells Anna to prepare a pyre, claiming she only wants to burn some things that Aeneas has left behind. That night, Dido reconsiders what she should do. She contemplates following the Trojans, but decides against it. She reaffirms her intention to commit suicide, motivated by guilt at having been unfaithful to the memory of Sychaeus.

Meanwhile, Aeneas is sleeping on the stern of his beached ship. Mercury comes down and tells him, in a dream, to leave right away. Aeneas wakes up and tells his men to sail immediately. They do. Then Dido wakes up and sees the Trojans leaving. She wishes she had killed Aeneas when she had the chance. She prays that his mission will fail, and that her people and his will become enemies. (We know from subsequent Roman history that her prayer will be answered in the form of the Punic Wars.) Then Dido sends her sister's old nurse to tell Anna to prepare the pyre. After Anna builds the pyre, Dido climbs on top of it and stabs herself with a sword that Aeneas gave to her. Anna climbs onto the pyre herself and tries to save the dying Dido, but it is too late. Juno sends down Iris, the messenger of the gods, to take a lock of Dido's hair and prepare her for death. Iris does this, and Dido dies.

Book V: Games and a Conflagration

As they are sailing away from Carthage, the Trojans see a huge bonfire on the shore; it is, of course, Dido's funeral pyre. After departing from Carthage, a storm comes up and the Trojans decide to head for land. They arrive in Sicily, exactly on the spot where they buried Anchises one year before. This is in the region of Sicily ruled by Acestes, another exile from Troy.

Aeneas declares a feast day and ritual commemoration of his father. He also says that in nine days they will hold athletic contests in Anchises' honor. While Aeneas is making ritual offerings to his father, a giant snake crawls out of Anchises' burial mound and curls up around it. Then it slithers around all the ritual objects, eats from the altar, and then heads back under the tomb. Aeneas wonders if the snake is a local god, or if it is the spirit of his father. He proceeds with the sacrifice anyway.

When the ninth day arrives, it is time for the athletic contests. Both Trojans and local Sicilians compete. The first event is a boat race. The idea is for the competitors, teams of rowers in long galleys, to sail out to sea, round a certain half-submerged rock designated as the turning point, and then be the first team to make it back to shore. Four ships compete. On the way out, the ship commanded by a man called Gyas is in the lead. He keeps telling his pilot, Menoetes, to come in close around the rock, but Menoetes is afraid of crashing, and thus makes a wide turn. This gives Cloanthus, the captain of the next ship, the opportunity to squeeze in between Gyas and the rock, making a sharper turn that puts him in the lead for the homestretch. Gyas is so upset that he throws Menoetes overboard and takes the tiller himself. Menoetes swims over to the rock and climbs on top of it. The two ships in the rear are commanded by Sergestus and Mnestheus. Sergestus is in front until he gets greedy, tries to cut the turn too close, and smashes his oars against the rock. Mnestheus rounds the turn ahead of him. Next Mnestheus passes Gyas, who is having trouble acting as captain and pilot at the same time. Now Mnestheus and Cloanthus are competing for first place. Cloanthus prays to the sea-gods for help. A number of gods appear to help him on his way to victory. Cloanthus comes in first, followed by Mnestheus, with Gyas coming after him, and Sergestus bringing up the rear in his disabled craft. Aeneas gives prizes to each of them.

The next event is a footrace. It looks like Nisus is going to win it, but then he slips in some blood left over from one of the sacrificial animals. When he falls, he makes sure to trip the man behind him, Salius, so his beloved Euryalus can speed ahead to victory. After the race, Salius and Nisus both demand consolation prizes. Aeneas obliges both of them.

Next comes boxing. The first challenger to stand up is a Trojan named Dares. For a long time, no one has the courage to take him on, but then, after some prodding, a Sicilian named Entellus steps up. The fight is fairly even at first, but then Entellus puts all his weight into a punch and ends up falling flat on his face. King Acestes comes and helps him up. The fight goes on, however, and now that Entellus' pride is hurt he starts pounding Dares mercilessly. Eventually, Aeneas steps in to stop the fight. He tells everyone that the gods must be supporting Entellus, and that their will must be followed. Entellus claims his prize, a bull. To prove how powerful he is, Entellus punches the creature between the horns, shattering its skull and killing it.

The next contest is archery. Aeneas raises the mast of a ship on the plain. To the top is tethered a bird, which flaps around helplessly. The idea is to shoot the bird. Hippocoön shoots first. He hits the mast, but misses the bird. Next, Mnestheus shoots. He misses the bird, but cuts the cord. The bird flutters away. Now it is Eurytion's turn. He is the brother of Pandarus, a famous Trojan archer who died in the war against the Greeks. After saying a prayer to the spirit of his brother, Eurytion takes aim, shoots, and hits the escaping bird. Last up is the Sicilian King Acestes, who now has nothing to shoot at. Just to prove he still has strength in him, he shoots an arrow into the air. In mid-flight, the arrow catches fire and turns into a shooting star. Aeneas gives Acestes first prize. Second prize goes to Eurytion, third to Mnestheus, and fourth to Hippocoön.

Next, the young men take part in a display of cavalry maneuvers. However, things take a turn for the worse. Determined to stir up trouble, Juno sends Iris, the messenger of the gods, down to where the Trojan women are gathered on the shore. There, they are lamenting the journeys that await them. Iris takes the form of a Trojan woman, Beroe. In this disguise, she stirs up the spirit of discontent among the women and tells them to burn the ships. Iris tells the Trojan women that Cassandra appeared to her in a dream, and instructed her to pass this message along to them.

Then Iris hurls a torch at one of the ships. One of the Trojan women, Pyrgo, shouts that the woman standing before them cannot be Beroe, who is ill; she has to be a goddess. Suddenly, Iris vanishes as she returns to the heavens. Although the women are at first confused about what to do, it is not long before they join in burning the ships.

When word reaches the men, Ascanius is the first to rush back to the shore, on horseback. The others come hurrying after. The women, ashamed of what they have done, disperse; it is too late for apologies: the ships are ablaze. In desperation, Aeneas prays to Jupiter: "Either save the ships or strike me dead with a lightning bolt." In response, Jupiter sends a storm and the rain quenches the fires. All but four ships are saved.

After this disturbing incident, Aeneas is confused about what to do. Nantes, a wise old Trojan, suggests that they should leave behind in Sicily the number of people the burned ships would have carried. They can leave the women and the elderly, who can establish a new city in Sicily. Aeneas is not sure about this, but then, in the sky, he sees the ghost of Anchises. The ghost tells him to follow Nantes' plan. He also informs Aeneas that a difficult war awaits them in Italy, so they should take only their toughest warriors. Finally, the ghost says that, before traveling to Italy, Aeneas will first have to visit the underworld, where he will learn the future of his people. He will also see his father's spirit, which is in Elysium, the abode of the blessed, not Tartarus, the black pit where the souls of evil men go. After this, the ghost of Anchises vanishes.

The next day, Aeneas takes up the proposal with Acestes, who accepts the idea of some of Aeneas' people remaining in his land. They make up a list of everyone who is staying behind, and Aeneas plots out their new city. A few days later, after much feasting together, Aeneas and the remaining ships depart. At this point, Venus, who has been watching everything, turns to Neptune and asks that Aeneas be granted safe passage to Italy. Neptune says that Aeneas will get there safely, only losing one man. Then he calms the sea.

That night, after a day of smooth sailing, the rowers are relaxing on their benches. Palinurus, the pilot, is still awake, making sure everything is running well. Then, suddenly, Somnus, the god of sleep, descends from the heavens and takes the form of Phorbas, another Trojan. In this disguise, he tries to convince Palinurus to go to sleep. Palinurus rejects the idea, but then Somnus shakes some dew off the magical bough he carries in his hand. This dew, from the River Lethe in the underworld, makes Palinurus very sleepy. Finally, Palinurus tumbles overboard, breaking off a piece of the stern and rudder and taking them with him. He calls for help but no one hears him.

The ship sails on, and a little while later is passing by the rocks where the

Sirens are. Aeneas hears the surf breaking off the rocks, and takes the helm. He laments the loss of his friend, Palinurus, but blames him for trusting too much in a calm sea.

Book VI: The World Below

Aeneas arrives in Italy and stops first at the cave of the Sibyl, a prophetess who owes her power to the god Apollo. When Aeneas arrives at her temple, built by the famous inventor Daedalus, Aeneas spends some time admiring the doors of the temple. These doors depict various mythological scenes. Something they do not show is the death of Daedalus' son Icarus. Virgil tells us that Daedalus twice tried to fashion a depiction of his son's death in gold, but both times, he was overcome by emotion.

Then out of the temple comes Achates, who has gone ahead with the Sibyl. The Sibyl tells Aeneas to stop admiring the doors and sacrifice seven young bulls and seven ewes. Aeneas passes along the orders to his men to carry out the Sibyl's instructions. Then, the Sibyl takes Aeneas and Achates into her inner shrine. There, she becomes possessed by the god Apollo, and instructs Aeneas to pray. After that, the Sibyl offers some prophecies. Specifically, she says that Aeneas and his men will have to fight a war to secure their territory in Italy. She predicts that a new Achilles will arise in the territory of Latium. (Achilles was the greatest of the Greek warriors fighting against Troy in the Trojan War.) The Sibyl then says that this war will arise because of a foreign bride. She also says that the Trojans will find safety from an unexpected source: a Greek city.

After receiving this prophecy, Aeneas prays to be allowed to descend to the underworld, so that he can visit his father. The Sibyl says that the way down to the underworld is easy; it is coming back that is difficult. (Lewis depicts the journey of Puddleglum, Eustace, and Jill into the underworld in the same way in *The Silver Chair*; it is easy for them to go down but hard for them to return to the "sunlit lands".)

The Sibyl tells Aeneas that he must go deep into the forest and, in the darkest and most secluded part, find a tree sprouting a golden bough. He must pluck this bough and bring it as a gift to Proserpina, the queen of the underworld. The Sibyl says that only those who are destined to do so may pluck the bough; it cannot be taken by force.

Next, the Sibyl reveals a problem: the Trojans have become defiled and have to purify themselves. This is because one of their men has died and remains unburied. The Sibyl says they have to find out who it is, bury him, and then sacrifice some black animals. Then Aeneas can go down to the underworld.

The unburied dead man turns out to be Misenus. He had apparently made the mistake of thinking he was better at blowing his conch shell than the sea-god Triton. Triton's response was to drown Misenus in the surf.

While the Trojans start building a pyre for Misenus, Aeneas prays for a sign that the Sibyl's other predictions will come true, just as this one did. Venus sends down two doves, reassuring Aeneas. Then Aeneas asks to be shown where the golden bough is. The doves fly off and he follows. Eventually, they lead him to the right spot.

Aeneas is overjoyed, and breaks the bough off the tree. The bough clings to the tree a bit. Does this mean that Aeneas is acting against fate? (Generations of Virgil scholars have not been able to agree on the answer.)

Now armed with the golden bough, Aeneas follows the Sibyl down into the underworld. They come to the banks of the River Styx, where a crowd of souls has assembled, waiting to be ferried across by Charon, the boatman of the underworld. The Sibyl explains that only those who have been buried can cross; those who have not been buried must first wait a hundred years on the banks of the Styx.

At this point, Aeneas catches sight of his lost pilot, Palinurus, who is one of the unburied dead crowding the bank of the river. Aeneas asks Palinurus if Apollo's oracle had lied, and some god had killed him. Palinurus explains that no god killed him; rather, his rudder broke while he was leaning on it, and he fell into the water. Then Palinurus says he swam ashore, but some local people killed him.

Palinurus asks Aeneas to bury him, or to take him across the river. However, the Sibyl interrupts, saying once again that they cannot take any unburied people across the river. The good news is that some other locals are going to bury Palinurus soon enough. Palinurus is satisfied with this response.

Charon, the ferryman, approaches and asks Aeneas and the Sibyl what they want. The Sibyl explains that Aeneas is going to visit his father. Then she reveals the golden bough. Charon immediately takes them across the river Styx. Once they arrive on the other side, Aeneas and the Sibyl see various dead people.

Aeneas sees Dido, and approaches her. He tells her he is sorry, and how it was not his fault for leaving her: he was only doing the gods' bidding, just as he is now. However, Dido does not listen to him. Instead, without a word, she runs off to join the shade of her dead husband, Sychaeus.

Next, Aeneas sees some dead Trojan warriors, and some Greeks who scatter when he approaches. Then he catches sight of Deiphobus, a Trojan warrior. Deiphobus' face reveals that he has been cruelly mutilated. Deiphobus, who had married Helen after the death of Paris, says that his wife is to blame. During the fall of Troy, she let her former husband, Menelaus, and Ulysses into their bedroom, and the two of them beat him up. Deiphobus asks what Aeneas is doing there, but before he can answer, the Sibyl says that they must move on.

In their onward journey, Aeneas and the Sibyl come to a place where the road forks. The path on the left leads to Tartarus, the black pit of hell. The one on the right leads toward Elysium, where the blessed dead go. The Sibyl tells Aeneas about the horrible torments suffered by the souls in Tartarus. Rather than go there, Aeneas and the Sibyl go to the gates of Proserpina's palace where, after performing a cleansing ritual, Aeneas leaves the golden bough. After that, he and the Sibyl go to Elysium.

They approach Musaeus, an ancient singer and poet, and ask where Anchises is. Musaeus directs them to the spot. There they find Anchises watching the souls preparing for rebirth. Aeneas and Anchises share a tearful reunion (much like Tirian and his father when they meet in the new Narnia in *The Last Battle*). Then Aeneas catches sight of the thousands of souls crowding around a nearby river. He asks Anchises who these people are. Anchises explains that these are souls waiting to be reborn. They are drinking from the River Lethe, whose waters will wipe clean their memory of their previous lives. (This scene is reminiscent of the scene in *The Silver Chair* where Aslan raises King Caspian's dead body from a river.) Aeneas asks why these people would want to live again. Anchises explains that everything that exists, including the sky, the land, the water, the moon, sun, and stars, as well as living creatures, are all permeated with Spirit. This Spirit occasionally becomes part of living things. When this happens, though, the body pollutes the spirit and clouds its vision. Even in death, the spirit retains traces of its old life. As a result, the souls of the dead must spend a good deal of time (sometimes up to a thousand years) being purified; sometimes this process involves torment, so that they can regain clear vision. Those who were especially pure in life, like Anchises, get to go to Elysium. Then, when the time comes, the souls of the dead get to drink from the waters of Lethe and enter a new body.

Anchises shows Aeneas some of the people waiting to be reborn. These include many future leaders of Rome. First, Anchises points out a group of Aeneas' immediate descendents. Then he points out members of the Julian dynasty, culminating in Caesar Augustus. Then Anchises and Aeneas see various other figures from Roman history, last of whom is Marcellus, Augustus' nephew, son-in-law, and prospective heir. Anchises explains that Marcellus is destined to die young, without fulfilling his promise.

After this, Anchises shows Aeneas further glimpses of the future. Then he sees Aeneas off to his departure from the Underworld through the Gates of Sleep. There are two gates, to be precise. One, made of horn, is the gate from which "true shades" emerge. The other is made of ivory; through it, "false dreams" make their way to humanity. Aeneas and the Sibyl leave through the ivory gate of false dreams.

Once again, scholars are mystified by the meaning of this. Why does Aeneas go through the gate of ivory and not the gate of horn? Lewis, in his copy of the works of Virgil, offers five alternative explanations. Because:

1. Aeneas is not a spirit, that is, not a true spirit. (See line 894.)
2. Aeneas is not a sleeper, not a true sleeper.
3. All dreams, before midnight, are fake: only the ivory gate is open before midnight, and it is then that Aeneas emerges.
4. Virgil does not claim that his account of Hades is true.
5. This world is only a dream and Aeneas himself becomes unreal on re-entering it.

Book VII: Juno Served by a Fury
The Trojans hold a funeral for Aeneas' nurse, Caieta, who has died. Then, when the sea is calm, they set out. The moon is bright, so they can sail easily by night. As they approach the island of the sorceress Circe (who we know from Homer's *Odyssey*) the Trojans hear the sounds of wild animals. These animals used to be human beings, before they were transformed by Circe's power. Neptune sends the Trojans a favorable breeze so that they can pass by Circe's island safely.

When dawn breaks, Aeneas catches sight of a forest on the distant shoreline. There, a river (the Tiber) is spilling into the sea and a number of beautiful birds are flying around. Aeneas decides to head for land.

Next, Virgil calls on the Muse to help him set the scene of what is going on in Latium (the area around Rome) at the time in which the story is set. The king of Latium at the time of Aeneas' arrival is Latinus. He is old and has no male heir. All he has is one daughter, Lavinia. All of the most eligible bachelors of the region are competing for her hand. The most handsome is Turnus, whom Latinus' wife, Amata, thinks is perfect for their daughter. However, a number of strange omens have made Latinus uncertain about the match. Finally, Latinus consults the most prestigious oracle in the region, a holy waterfall. The waterfall tells him that his daughter is destined to marry a foreigner, and their descendents will rule the world. Thus, Latinus decides that marriage between Lavinia and Turnus is out of the question.

Latinus does not keep this news to himself. When Aeneas arrives, the whole region knows about the prophecy of the holy waterfall. Once the Trojans disembark, they enjoy a feast; they lay out on the grass hard wheaten cakes as platters for their meal; then they devour the cakes. Ascanius shouts out: "Look, how we've devoured our tables even!" This fulfills the prophecy of Celaeno the Harpy from Book III: that the Trojans will not be safe until their hunger has reduced them to gnawing on their tables. Aeneas immediately recognizes the sign, and tells his companions that this is their destined homeland. For some reason, he also tells his fellow Trojans that he knows this because of a prophecy his father told him, not because of the prophecy of the Harpy Celaeno.

The Trojans proceed to host a festival in honor of the gods, and Jupiter thunders jovially in response. The next day they go out exploring, and Aeneas sends emissaries to King Latinus. In the meantime, Aeneas begins to build a fortress in case there is conflict with the inhabitants of the land. When the emissaries reach Latinus, he tells them that he knows who they are. He also says that his own people are descended from the god Saturn and are naturally just. Then he shows that he knows the tale of Dardanus, an ancient ancestor of the Trojans, who came from Italy (we learned about him in Book III).

In response, the Trojan envoys explain how they are descended from Dardanus and have come to Italy on a mission from the gods. They ask permission to settle on the coast, and offer Latinus gifts of friendship.

After thinking it over, Latinus says that he will accept the offer. Not only this, but he also reveals the prophecy that his daughter must marry a foreigner. He says that Aeneas is the man. Then Latinus sends them back with some new horses, including a semi-immortal horse for Aeneas.

Everything seems to be going smoothly until Juno appears on the scene. She does not like what she sees. Even though she knows that Aeneas has fate on his side, she determines to make things difficult for him. She decides to start a war between the Trojans and the Latins. To do this, she goes down to Hades and arouses Allecto, a terrible Fury. Allecto goes to the palace of Latinus and seeks out Amata, Latinus' wife and the mother of Lavinia. Allecto plucks one of the snakes that grows out of her own head instead of hair and throws it at Amata. Invisibly, it makes its way inside her body and infects her with hatred.

Amata pleads with Latinus *not* to allow Aeneas to marry their daughter. However, Latinus does not listen. Therefore, Amata takes her daughter and journeys into the woods, where she lives as a Bacchante, a devotee of Bacchus, the god of drunkenness and ecstasy. As word travels around the region about Amata's activities, many women decide to join her. One day, standing among the other Bacchantes and holding a burning pine torch, Amata sings a wedding hymn for Turnus and Lavinia. Then she incites the other women to join in her crazed revelry.

Meanwhile, Allecto travels to the town of the Rutulians, the people of Turnus. She finds Turnus in his bedroom and appears to him in a dream in the form of an old woman. In this shape, she tells him that he is in the wrong for allowing his prospective bride to get away from him. She says he should go make war against the Trojans but keep peace with the Latins. Turnus says that he will make war but tells Allecto to leave him alone. Allecto does not like Turnus' tone. She becomes enraged, pulls two snakes out of her head and starts cracking them like a whip. Then she hurls a torch at Turnus. He wakes up in a fright but finds himself alone. Turnus immediately decides upon war with the Trojans, and instructs his soldiers to march toward King Latinus' capital. The other Rutulians agree with his plan.

Next, Allecto visits the Trojans and finds Ascanius hunting. She puts his hounds on the scent of a deer. What the hounds and Ascanius do not know is that this deer has been domesticated by Tyrrhus, the warden of King Latinus' estates. After Ascanius shoots the deer with his arrow and it runs, mortally wounded, back to its house, a huge battle erupts between the Trojans and the Latin herdsmen and their associates. Some people die in the conflict.

Allecto returns to Juno to report on her accomplishments. Juno takes over and sends Allecto back down to Hades. By this time, the battle has broken up between the Latin shepherds and the Trojans. The Latins return to their city with their dead. Turnus is in the city now, and he incites the crowd, telling them of Latinus' plans to marry off Lavinia to a Trojan. Turnus, of course, says that he should be the one to marry Lavinia since he is not a foreigner. All those whose relatives have joined Amata in her wild revelry in the woods are the first to join in the call for war. King Latinus refuses to give in, but is unable to stop his citizens' frenzy. He predicts that the people, led by Turnus, will be punished for acting against the will of the gods.

Virgil tells us that the Latins, like the Romans of his own day, have a custom that, whenever war is declared, they open a pair of ceremonial gates locked with a hundred bolts. The people call upon Latinus to open these gates but he refuses. Thus, Juno comes down and opens the gates herself. Throughout the Italian countryside, men prepare for war against the Trojans. Then Virgil, like Homer before him, calls upon the Muses to help him list the warriors on the Italian side. Most notable among them are Mezentius of Tuscany, "who held the gods in scorn." There is also Mezentius' son, Lausus, the most handsome man in Italy except for Turnus. Another warrior is of course Turnus himself, wearing an impressive suit of armor. Finally, there is the fearsome female warrior, Camilla, who is so fast that she can run over the top of a wheat field without crushing the stalks, or over the top of the sea.

Book VIII: Arcadian Allies

Turnus and his allies are having huge success rounding up local recruits against the foreign invaders. They also send out emissaries to the Greek hero Diomedes (a famous figure from Homer's *Iliad*), trying to convince him to take up the fight against his old enemies, the Trojans.

Aeneas has a good idea of what is going on, and is deep in thought about what to do in response. All that thinking makes him tired and so he falls asleep. In his sleep, Aeneas sees Tiberinus, the god of the River Tiber, appear before him. Tiberinus tells him that the gods are not angry with him anymore, and that he should not be afraid of the war to come. Then Tiberinus tells Aeneas that he is going to find, under some trees by the shore, a white sow nursing thirty piglets. This will serve as confirmation that after thirty years Ascanius will found a city called Alba. This is a reiteration of the prophecy made to Aeneas in Book III. Next, Tiberinus gives Aeneas some helpful advice. He tells him to go to the nearby kingdom of the Arcadians, a Greek tribe, ruled by a man named Evander. He says that these men are always at war with the Rutulians; Aeneas should bring them on his side. Finally, he urges Aeneas to pray to Juno, to try to win her over.

Aeneas wakes up, gives thanks to the god, and then orders his men to make ready two ships. However, at that moment, Aeneas catches sight of the white sow and her litter; he decides to sacrifice them to Juno. Then Tiberinus makes the waters of the River Tiber perfectly still, so the ships can sail easily to the settlement of the Arcadians.

The Arcadians are offering a sacrifice to Hercules; when they see the Trojans arrive, King Evander's son Pallas runs down to ask them who they are. Aeneas explains his mission and Pallas invites them to dine with his family that night. Then Aeneas approaches Evander and tells him of their common ancestry and that they have a shared enemy: the Rutulians. Aeneas urges Evander to join him in battle.

Evander offers to Aeneas the support of his troops and then they enjoy a feast together. After they are finished eating, Evander points to a collapsed cave on the side of a nearby mountain, and begins to tell a story. The cave was formerly inhabited by a half-beast, half-man, named Cacus, who breathed fire and killed many. His father was Vulcan, the god of fire. Then Evander explains that Hercules came and attacked Cacus. In the process, he ripped out the side of the mountain, because Cacus was hiding inside. That is why the Arcadians now worship Hercules as their special god.

When the feast is finished, the Arcadians continue their rituals. The Salii, a certain class of priest, come in and begin to dance in worship of Hercules and sing a song about their hero. After this, the people walk back to the city. Evander walks with Aeneas and tells him about how the land used to be in ancient times. Evander reveals various sites, including sacred grottoes, which Virgil explains will be important in later Roman history and myth. When they get to Evander's settlement, which is also the future site of Rome, Evander invites Aeneas to make himself at home. Aeneas does so and falls asleep.

Meanwhile, Venus, lying in bed beside her husband Vulcan, is troubled by these events. Putting on her most seductive voice, she convinces Vulcan to make some special armor for Aeneas. Vulcan does so.

At dawn, Evander wakes up and goes outside, accompanied by his son, Pallas. He finds Aeneas, accompanied by Achates, and they sit down for a conversation. Evander tells Aeneas that the Arcadians themselves are not going to be strong enough allies against Turnus and his men. He suggests that the nearby Etrurians might offer additional support.

At one time, Mezentius tyrannically ruled the Etrurians. However, they ejected him as their ruler and so Mezentius became an ally of Turnus. There are thousands of Etrurians ready for action, but a sign that they were given holds them back; the sign indicated they should only go to war under a foreign commander. Obviously, Aeneas is the one to whom the sign was pointing.

Evander suggests that Aeneas should command the Etrurians, along with a contingent of Arcadians. He also offers his son, Pallas, to teach Aeneas more about warfare. When Evander finishes his speech, they hear thunder from the heavens. Aeneas says that this sound indicates his armor is being made ready for him. Evander and Aeneas now make the proper sacrifices, in preparation for war. Some riders are dispatched to get the Etrurians; a ship sails down the Tiber to let Ascanius know what is happening, and Aeneas chooses his fighting force from among the Arcadians. Before the army departs, Evander takes Pallas aside and tells him how he wishes he were young and could go in his stead. He prays to the gods to protect his son. Then the army departs.

On their way, Venus meets them. She approaches Aeneas and gives him the weapons made by Vulcan. Aeneas admires the armor, especially the shield, on which Vulcan has fashioned many scenes from future Roman history. These include scenes immediately preceding the time of Virgil's writing, such as Caesar Augustus' defeat of the allied forces of Marc Antony and Cleopatra. Even though Aeneas does not know fully what these pictures mean, he is encouraged by them and takes up his shield.

Book IX: A Night Sortie, a Day Assault

Book IX begins with Juno sending Iris down to Turnus to tell him that it is time to go to war against the Trojans. Therefore, Turnus gets his men ready and marches out. From their fort, the Trojans (except for Aeneas who is still conversing with Evander) see Turnus and his forces approaching. When Turnus arrives, he immediately rides around the fort, looking for a means of entrance. Finding none, he decides to lure the Trojans out of their fort by setting fire to their fleet.

Virgil asks the gods which one of them saved the ships. The answer to this question comes in the form of a flashback. At the time when the Trojans left Troy, the earth goddess Cybele (here portrayed as the mother of Jupiter) asked her son to keep the Trojans' ships safe forever. Cybele's son had built the ships from a forest that Cybele especially cherished. She wanted to ensure the lasting survival of her forest, even if that forest was used to make ships. Jupiter assured her that once the ships completed their voyage, he would turn them into goddesses. Therefore, that is what happens when Turnus and his men try to burn the fleet. The ships turn into beautiful women and depart into the sea. Turnus puts his own spin on this event. He tells his men that this is a sign that the gods want to prevent the Trojans from escaping. After taunting the Trojans, Turnus declares an end to fighting for the day, and he allows his troops to eat.

Meanwhile, the Trojan warriors Nisus and Euryalus are guarding their camp. Nisus tells Euryalus his plan to go out to find Aeneas and bring him back to the Trojan camp. Euryalus wants to accompany his lover, but Nisus is reluctant to allow this because he will need someone to bury him if he dies. Euryalus insists on joining Nisus anyway.

Nisus and Euryalus report their plan to the Trojan council who are pleased with the idea. Ascanius promises great reward if they are successful. Euryalus simply requests that the Trojans care for his mother if he dies.

Nisus and Euryalus commence their journey. When they reach the Rutulian camp, they kill a group of men in their sleep. They continue on their way after Euryalus takes a helmet as booty. Soon, their enemies ride past on horseback; the moonlight flashing off Euryalus' helmet attracts their attention. The cavalrymen shout at the two Trojans, who flee into the woods. The Rutulians surround the wood, but Nisus escapes.

When Nisus realizes that Euryalus is not with him, he goes back to rescue him. He finds Euryalus being attacked by a large group of Rutulians. After debating in his mind what he should do, Nisus says a quick prayer and throws his spear. He kills one man. Then he throws another spear and kills another one. Then Volcens, one of the Rutulians, decides to kill Euryalus. Nisus, in desperation, shouts out from his hiding place, trying to distract the enemy. However, it is too late. Volcens stabs Euryalus and kills him.

Enraged, Nisus runs into the midst of his opponents. He succeeds in killing Volcens, but dies at the hands of the other Rutulians, falling on the body of his beloved Euryalus. The Rutulians carry Volcens back to their camp, plus the bodies of the two dead Trojans. Once they arrive there, the Rutulians lament the deaths of their own men whom the Trojan pair slaughtered.

At dawn, Turnus organizes his men. They march on the Trojan fort, carrying Nisus and Euryalus' heads atop their spears. When the Trojans see the skewered heads of their dead comrades, they begin weeping. Soon, rumor of what has happened makes its way to Euryalus' mother, who is naturally overcome with grief.

Turnus' men attack the Trojan ramparts, interlocking their shields in a tortoise formation. However, the Trojans drive them back. After some more fighting, Turnus throws a torch and sets one of the Trojan towers on fire. Eventually the tower collapses. There are only two survivors: Helenor, who launches himself at the Rutulians and is immediately killed, and Lycus, who tries to make his way back into the Trojan camp over the wall. Turnus catches Lycus and pulls him down; he rips off some of the wall in the process. The battle continues.

Next, a Rutulian named Numanus steps forward and taunts the Trojans, calling them women. Ascanius prays to Jupiter, who thunders from the sky. Then Ascanius shoots Numanus through the head. This is the first man he has ever killed in combat. For this deed, the god Apollo (who is himself an archer) praises Ascanius. Then Apollo comes down and stands beside Ascanius in the form of Butes, an old Trojan. In this disguise, he praises Ascanius, but encourages him to stay out of the battle from henceforth. Apollo returns to heaven, and everyone recognizes that a god has spoken to Ascanius. The Trojans keep Ascanius out of the battle as the fight rages on.

Now, two Trojans, Pandarus and Bitias, open a gate and dare their enemies to come in. The Rutulians storm the entrance, but the Trojans push them back once again. Then Turnus kills various Trojans, including Bitias. Seeing his brother killed, Pandarus shuts the gate with Turnus inside the Trojan fortress. Undaunted, Turnus dares the Trojans to fight him, boasting that he is a new Achilles. Someone throws a spear at Turnus, but Juno deflects it. Then Turnus kills a number of men until Mnestheus shouts at the Trojans, encouraging them to kill Turnus. The Trojans attack Turnus and drive him against the River Tiber, which functions as one of the boundary lines of their camp. Juno does not dare to give Turnus sufficient strength to take on that many men because that would be too great an interference from the gods. Jupiter tells Iris to tell Juno to give up. Unable to hold out any longer, Turnus casts himself into the Tiber where he is carried safely by the current to the other side.

Book X: The Death of Princes

Jupiter has been watching the battle unfold between the Rutulians and the Trojans. When all the other gods are assembled, he asks them why peace is not possible. Venus speaks up for the Trojans, saying they have suffered enough; if Jupiter plans to destroy them, he should just go ahead with his plan, but he should at least let Ascanius survive, even if he will live out the rest of his life ingloriously. Alternatively, Venus suggests Jupiter should let the Trojans go back and resettle Troy. Next Juno claims the battle was not her fault and that Jupiter could have stepped in earlier to fix things. Having now heard both sides, Jupiter decides to stay out of the fight. Thus, the battle between the two sides continues.

That night, Aeneas sails back down the river to rejoin his companions. Since we last saw him meeting with Evander, he has gone to see the Etruscan

King Tarchon. He has brought Tarchon, along with thirty ships filled with Etruscan warriors as allies. As they sail on through the night, Aeneas remains awake at the tiller. A group of nymphs swims by his ship, the same nymphs that used to be his fleet, before they were magically transformed. The nymphs let Aeneas know about the difficult situation in which Ascanius finds himself. Then the nymphs give Aeneas an added push to hurry him down the river.

The next morning, when the Trojans see Aeneas, their spirits revive. Turnus is excited too, because he sees an opportunity to bring the fight to the Trojans on the landing-ground. Meanwhile, Tarchon urges his fleet to drive their ships up onto land. Everybody executes this maneuver successfully except for Tarchon himself; his ship splits in half on a sandbar, and many of his men are carried away by the undertow.

Scarcely any time passes before the Trojans are fighting the Rutulians on the beach. Aeneas kills many and there is much slaughter carried out by both armies. At a certain point, the Arcadians retreat since they are accustomed to fighting on horseback rather than on foot. Pallas shouts at them, telling them they have to keep fighting. The sea is behind the Arcadians; thus, they have nowhere to go. Rather than retreat, Pallas rushes into the fight and kills various men. The Arcadians are encouraged by Pallas' speech and behavior, and regain their courage. In the midst of the battle, Pallas is fighting Lausus, the son of the Rutulian ally Mezentius. When his sister, the nymph Juturna, tells Turnus to go help Lausus, he does so. When he gets to where the two young warriors are fighting, he announces that he has come to kill Pallas, and that he wishes Pallas' father Evander were there to watch.

At Turnus' command, the other soldiers back away. Pallas challenges Turnus, and before throwing his spear, Pallas prays to Hercules, the god of the Arcadians, for help. Hercules hears him, but is powerless to do anything. Jupiter tells Hercules that no one can escape fate. (Jupiter's own son, Sarpedon, was killed at Troy.) Besides, Jupiter says, Turnus will die soon anyway. Pallas throws his spear with all his strength, but it merely grazes Turnus. Then Turnus throws his spear and it strikes a mortal blow against Pallas. As Turnus stands over Pallas' body, he promises that his fallen enemy will be afforded all proper funeral rites. Then he takes Pallas' ornamented belt.

When Aeneas hears of Pallas' death, he is enraged. He kills many of the enemy warriors around him; then he captures four men alive so that he can sacrifice them at Pallas' funeral. Next, Magus falls at Aeneas' knees and begs him for mercy. However, Aeneas refuses and stabs him in the throat. Then Aeneas chases down a priest wearing holy robes and kills him too. Aeneas proceeds to kill many others, including Tarquitus who also begs him for mercy. Next, Aeneas addresses Lucagus who was attacking him in a chariot driven by his brother Liger. Aeneas kills Liger by spearing him in the groin.

Then he drags Lucagus from the chariot and kills him, despite Lucagus' pleas for mercy. The battle continues. After a little while, Ascanius and the other Trojans are able to come out of the fort because the arrival of Aeneas and his allies has taken the pressure off them.

Meanwhile, Jupiter is watching the battle. He tells Juno that Venus is helping the Trojans. Juno asks that Turnus' life be spared so he can see his father, Daunus, again. Jupiter agrees to this. Juno is pleased. She returns to earth where she makes a "stunt double" of Aeneas. She sends this stunt double out into the front lines of battle. When Turnus catches sight of it, he throws his spear at it, but the stunt double dodges it. Then Aeneas' double turns and flees from the battle. Thinking he has Aeneas on the run, Turnus runs after him. Aeneas' double runs onto a ship moored nearby. This is the ship King Osinius, one of Aeneas' Etruscan allies, sailed from Clusium. Aeneas' double hides on board the ship. Turnus runs after him. Just then, Juno snaps the cable that is holding the ship to the shoreline and the ship rolls away on the surf.

Meanwhile, the real Aeneas calls out for Turnus to come back and fight. At this point, Aeneas' stunt double shoots up to the heavens, and Turnus realizes he has been tricked. In his shame, Turnus prays that the ship will come to ground on an empty coast and he contemplates committing suicide.

Meanwhile, Mezentius, the fearsome Rutulian ally, is killing many of the Trojans. When Mezentius gives a mortal wound to Orodes, the dying man predicts Mezentius' imminent death. After the fight rages on for some time, Aeneas and Mezentius finally meet in combat. Mezentius throws his spear but it bounces off Aeneas' shield and stabs another soldier in the groin. Then Aeneas throws his spear and it punctures Mezentius' shield and stabs him in the groin. As Mezentius backs away slowly with this horrible wound, his son Lausus heroically comes to the rescue. This inspires many Rutulians to come to Mezentius' defense, and Aeneas is pushed back. Eventually, Lausus and Aeneas engage one another in battle; Aeneas stabs him through his flimsy shield. However, as soon as he sees Lausus fall, Aeneas is moved by pity; he promises to give Lausus back to his family for burial, without taking any booty from his body. Then he tells Lausus' fellow soldiers to retrieve his corpse.

Over by the river, Mezentius has washed his wound and is lying against a tree. When he sees his son's body brought to him on a shield, he is overwhelmed by grief, and realizes he must soon die himself. However, first, he gets on his horse and rides back to the battle. Eventually, he finds Aeneas, and they engage in single combat. Aeneas brings Mezentius down by spearing his horse in the head. Pinned under the animal, Mezentius cannot escape. He asks Aeneas to bury him in the same grave with his son. Then Aeneas kills Mezentius.

Lewis' Top Ten

Book XI: Debaters and a Warrior Girl

Although the death of Pallas has disturbed him, Aeneas makes offerings to the gods as a sign of thanks for his victory. Then he addresses his soldiers. He seeks to encourage them by telling them that the lion's share of their work is over. Next, he instructs them to bury the dead. He orders that they should send Pallas' body back to his father Evander. Aeneas goes to the shelter where Pallas' body lies and he weeps over the slain warrior. He is especially sad for having failed in his promise to Evander to keep Pallas safe. Virgil now describes Pallas' funeral procession as it takes form. The procession includes the four prisoners Aeneas intends to have sacrificed over Pallas' pyre.

When Aeneas returns to camp, he finds that emissaries from the Latins have arrived; they ask for a day of truce to bury their dead. Aeneas agrees to this but upbraids them for allowing Turnus to turn their hearts against the Trojans. Aeneas suggests that Turnus should have remained in the battle so that he could kill him. Then Drances, a Latin elder, speaks up. He tells Aeneas that they will get rid of Turnus as an ally and make peace again with the Trojans. Thus, the Trojans and Latins agree to a twelve-day truce.

Pallas' funeral procession reaches the city of the Arcadians. King Evander, overcome with grief, throws himself on his son's body. Evander makes a lengthy lamentation. He wishes he had died instead of his son. However, he does not blame Aeneas for Pallas' death.

The next morning, the Trojans burn their dead. When the third day of the truce arrives, the Trojans bury the ashes and bones. That same day, in the city of the Latins, mothers lament the loss of their sons. Some of them say that they should sever their alliance with Turnus. Drances supports this, but Queen Amata, who still wants Turnus, not Aeneas, as a son-in-law, does not agree to this plan.

At this moment, the emissaries return from the Greek King Diomedes. (These emissaries were sent out at the beginning of Book VIII to gain Diomedes' help in the war against the Trojans.) The emissaries report that Diomedes has refused to help them. King Latinus wants to hear the full story, so he calls an assembly and orders the emissaries to address it. They report what Diomedes has told them: that he has suffered enough fighting against the Trojans at Troy. He suggests the Latins should take the gifts they were offering him and present them to Aeneas instead.

After hearing this report, King Latinus addresses the assembly and reveals what he heard from the oracle in Book VII, that the Trojans are destined to rule Italy. He says that there is no point in fighting them; the Latins should either: join them as a single people, or, if the Trojans choose to leave, they should help them build a fleet.

Next, Drances speaks up. He says that Latinus should go a step further and promise his daughter Lavinia in marriage to Aeneas. Then he addresses Turnus, who apparently is present at the meeting. He tells Turnus to renounce his claim to Lavinia's hand. If Turnus refuses to do this, then he should fight Aeneas for Lavinia's hand in single combat.

In reply, Turnus derides Drances for his own unwillingness to fight the Trojans and for thinking that the Latins cannot win against the Trojans in an all-out war. Then Turnus addresses Latinus. He tells him that they still have enough allies to fight the Trojans. However, if it is to be single combat between he and Aeneas, then he is ready.

While the Latins are debating what to do, Aeneas and his army have marched into the plain. A messenger enters the Latin city and alerts the people, who arm for battle. In the assembly, Turnus takes Aeneas' action as proof that seeking peace is useless. He orders his captains to prepare for war.

The city is quickly fortified. At the same time, Amata, Lavinia, and the other prominent women of the city proceed to the shrine of Minerva; the women pray to Minerva, asking her to keep their city safe.

Turnus arms for battle. When he emerges, he meets Camilla, the Volscian warrior queen, riding up with her battalions. Turnus is glad to see Camilla. He tells her to engage Aeneas, while he and his men set an ambush to catch the Trojans in a wooded mountain pass. Turnus informs Camilla that she will have the forces of Messapus to assist her in battle against Aeneas.

Meanwhile in heaven, the goddess of the hunt, Diana, speaks to Opis, one of her serving maidens (and a goddess herself). Diana explains how Camilla's father, Metabus, was an exiled king who raised his daughter in the woods, taking on Diana as his child's patroness. Diana gives Opis an arrow, instructing her that whoever kills Camilla should be killed, in turn, with the arrow.

By this time, the Trojans are approaching the city of the Latins. Camilla and Messapus are in the plain waiting to meet them. The battle begins. Camilla kills many Trojans. However, at a certain point in the battle, Camilla chases Arruns, who is wearing some fancy clothes. Virgil tells us that Camilla has fallen prey to "a girl's love of finery." Finally, Arruns turns to face Camilla. He prays to Apollo before throwing his spear, saying that he does not expect any glory for killing a woman but that he needs to stop her from killing all of the Trojans. As we soon find out: Apollo grants Arruns' request to be successful in killing Camilla, but not his request to return home safely.

Arruns throws his spear and strikes Camilla in her one exposed breast; then he runs away. Camilla asks her friend Acca to help her as she slips from the saddle and dies. As planned, Diana's servant Opis draws an arrow, takes aim, and shoots Arruns, killing him.

After the death of Camilla, the Latins retreat into the city. A bottleneck is created at the city gates and the Trojans press in behind them. Many are killed in the furious slaughter. Eventually, the Latins seal up their city. When news reaches Turnus, where he is still waiting to ambush Aeneas in the mountain pass, he is dismayed. He leads his soldiers away from their planned place of ambush and heads toward the town. Then Aeneas and his own contingent, which has not yet arrived at the scene of the battle, march through the undefended pass and make their way toward the town. The two armies see each other. Turnus' men want to engage Aeneas and his army in battle, but the sun is setting. Thus, Turnus and his men retreat into the city for the night while Aeneas and his men lie in wait upon the plain.

Book XII: The Fortunes of War

Turnus announces that the time has come for him to fight Aeneas in single combat. Latinus tries to convince Turnus to give up, to take some other woman as his wife and leave Lavinia to Aeneas. However, Turnus refuses. Then Amata voices her opinion that she would rather kill herself than have Aeneas as a son-in-law. Lavinia has been listening to this exchange and blushes. Turnus, seeing her, feels overcome with love; he determines that he simply must fight Aeneas. Turnus readies his chariot and horses, and arms himself for battle. At the same time, Aeneas prepares for the conflict as well.

The next morning, the Latins emerge from their city. Both armies make room on the plain for the planned battle between the two champions. From a nearby height, Juno is watching these events. Standing beside her is Turnus' sister, the nymph Juturna. Juno tells Juturna that she has done all she can for Turnus. If Turnus is to be saved then it is up to Juturna to help him.

Down on the plain, the leaders from both sides are meeting. Aeneas prays and asserts that if Turnus wins, the Trojans will leave. However, if the Trojans win, Aeneas promises that they will not enslave the Latins, but rather ask them to join them as equal citizens in a new nation. Latinus agrees to these terms. They sacrifice animals to formalize their agreement.

However, the Rutulians are becoming worried. Now that they see the two champions ready for battle, they can easily see that Turnus is not strong enough to beat Aeneas. Knowing what the Rutulians are thinking, Juturna descends among them, taking the form of the warrior Camers. She tries to stir them up to fight on behalf of Turnus. Just then, the Rutulians see an eagle, considered a representative of Jupiter, swoop down and seize a swan. Then, a number of other seabirds attack; eventually, the eagle must release the swan and retreat. Tolumnius, a soothsayer who can interpret the movements of birds, says that this is a sign that the Rutulians should assist Turnus. Then he throws his spear at the Trojans, killing one of nine brothers who are standing together. The brothers respond by seizing their weapons and racing forward to do battle with the Rutulians. Soon, both armies are fighting.

Aeneas tries to stop his men from fighting, but then somebody hits him with an arrow. When Turnus sees Aeneas falling back, he is thrilled. He moves his chariot into action and begins to kill many Trojans. Meanwhile, Iapyx, taught the healing arts by Apollo, tends to Aeneas' wound (like Lucy who is taught the healing arts by Aslan in *The Lion, the Witch and the Wardrobe*). The difficulty is that Iapyx cannot extract the arrowhead from Aeneas' body.

Venus moves into action again. She comes to Aeneas' aid with a special plant, called dittany, which she has plucked from Mount Ida in Crete. Venus mixes the essence of this plant, along with some other substances (like ambrosia, the food of the gods) in the water that Iapyx is using to cleanse Aeneas' wound. Venus' magic works and Iapyx is able easily to remove the arrowhead. Iapyx calls for Aeneas' armor and sends him into battle.

Aeneas leads the Trojans to attack their enemy and they kill many. Not pleased with this, Juturna knocks Turnus' charioteer, Metiscus, onto the ground. Then she takes his form and starts driving Turnus erratically over the battlefield, keeping him out of Aeneas' reach. Aeneas pursues Turnus as best he can. However, other enemy soldiers distract him. For a while, both Aeneas and Turnus fight in their own corners of the battlefield, each killing many opponents. Then Venus gives Aeneas an idea. Taking a stand on a hilltop overlooking the city, Aeneas announces to his captains that the time has come to level the city of the Latins. Thus, the Trojans attack the city.

Seeing the Trojans attack from her window, Amata thinks that Turnus must be dead. In grief, she hangs herself with cloth torn from her robe. Lavinia, learning of her mother's suicide, laments loudly, as does King Latinus. Turnus hears the commotion from the city. Juturna, still disguised as the charioteer Metiscus, tries to convince Turnus to keep killing Trojans on the edge of the battle. However, Turnus recognizes Juturna and refuses to follow her plan. Word comes to Turnus of the plight of the city and of the death of Amata. This strengthens Turnus' resolve to find and face Aeneas, even though he thinks he will die in the attempt.

When Aeneas hears that Turnus is coming, he stops attacking the city and goes out to face him. Both sides clear a space for the two champions to battle one another in single combat (like King Peter challenging Miraz to single combat in *Prince Caspian*); soon, Turnus and Aeneas are throwing spears at each other. Then they fight with swords. While they are fighting, Jupiter raises a scale. In it, he places each champion's destiny; whichever man's side of the scale sinks towards the ground, this will indicate which man will die.

Meanwhile, Turnus gives Aeneas a mighty blow with his sword, but the blade shatters on impact. Turnus was using Metiscus' sword, instead of his own and it was useless against Aeneas' divine armor. Turnus tries to retreat, but he is hemmed in by the Trojans, by the city walls, and by the marsh. As he runs, Turnus calls for his sword, but Aeneas warns Turnus' men that if they help Turnus, then he, Aeneas, will destroy their city. Aeneas approaches the olive tree stump where his spear is stuck fast. Seeing this, Turnus prays to the local gods, asking them to prevent Aeneas from being able to pull out his spear. The gods grant Turnus' request. Meanwhile, Juturna, disguised as Metiscus, gives Turnus his sword. Venus returns to the action, enabling Aeneas to pull his spear out of the stump.

Jupiter tells Juno that the end has come. He forbids her to interfere with Aeneas any more. Juno submits to Jupiter's decree, but she requests that when Aeneas and Lavinia marry, and their people become one, that the Latins will not have to give up their name. Jupiter agrees to this; then he sends one of the Furies to stop Juturna's meddling efforts. The fury changes into a bird and starts flapping around Turnus, annoying him. Juturna realizes what is going on, and she withdraws from the battle.

Finally, Aeneas and Turnus face off. They exchange hostile words. Then Turnus picks up a large rock to throw at Aeneas, but he is not strong enough to fling it far, and the stone falls short. Next, Aeneas throws his spear, puncturing Turnus' shield and stabbing him in the thigh. Turnus falls to the ground. He asks Aeneas to spare his life so that he can see his father again, and he gives up his claim to Lavinia. Aeneas debates in his mind what to do. However, he notices the belt that Turnus stole from the dead body of Pallas. Turnus is wearing it on his shoulder. Aeneas is enraged. He shouts that Pallas will now gain his revenge. Aeneas stabs Turnus, who quickly dies as his soul departs for the underworld.

CONCLUSION

In his Introduction to Sister Penelope's translation of St. Athanasius' *De Incarnatione Verbi Dei*, C. S. Lewis recommends the reading of old books. He suggests that when we want to understand Platonism we should turn first to Plato, not to some modern interpreter of him. If we want to have a clear understanding of "mere Christianity" then that too requires knowledge of the old books; it...

> ... puts the controversies of the moment in their proper perspective. Such a standard can be acquired only from the old books. It is a good rule, after reading a new book, never to allow yourself another new one till you have read an old one in between. If that is too much for you, you should at least read one old one to every three new ones.

> Every age has its own outlook. It is specially good at seeing certain truths and specially liable to make certain mistakes. We all, therefore, need the books that will correct the characteristic mistakes of our own period. And that means the old books.[428]

Now, from our perspective in the twenty-first century, all the books on Lewis' "top ten" list will appear to be old. Of course, it was not so from Lewis' own vantage point. It is interesting to note that on Lewis' list there were four authors from the twentieth century (Balfour, Otto, Chesterton, Williams), two from the nineteenth (MacDonald and Wordsworth), one from the eighteenth century (Boswell), one from the seventeenth century (Herbert), one from the sixth century (Boethius), and one from before the time of Christ (Virgil). Lewis obviously kept his own rule of granting priority to the reading of old books.

However, I anticipate that this brief survey of the first three books on Lewis' "top ten" list has probably raised certain questions. First, why did Lewis choose the particular books that he did? The question must be answered in the case of each individual volume. Obviously, *Phantastes*, as Lewis says, "baptized his imagination". It also started him on the road of reading all of MacDonald's works—a lifetime project that influenced Lewis' return to Christian faith and his nurturing in that faith. This was accomplished largely through MacDonald's imaginative works of fiction.

In the case of Chesterton, it was his non-fiction works, *The Everlasting Man* in particular, that influenced Lewis most, again in terms of his return to Christian faith. So did Lewis only include on his "top ten" list those books that influenced his faith? The inclusion of Virgil's *Aeneid* knocks out that suggestion. Rather than influencing a turn *toward* Christian faith, Virgil helped to bring about Lewis' early turn *away* from the Christian faith.

So how was Virgil an influence upon Lewis? To sum up our answer to this question we must first recall the original question that led Lewis to produce his "top ten" list. The question posed by *The Christian Century* was: "What books did most to shape your vocational attitude and your philosophy of life?" As anyone who is familiar at all with Lewis' works knows, he paid quite close attention to the meaning of words, even delivering lectures on the topic later published in book form as *Studies in Words*. Thus, I think in answering the question posed by *The Christian Century*, Lewis limited his answer to books that shaped, very specifically, his vocational attitude and his philosophy of life. For Lewis, the phrase "philosophy of life" would have encompassed matters of faith and religion. However, it was perhaps in terms of "vocation" that the *Aeneid* most influenced Lewis, as I have pointed out earlier. After all, the *Aeneid* is the great epic poem of vocation. This, perhaps, answers a related question: why did Lewis place Virgil on his "top ten" list and not Homer? Expanding upon the answer I gave earlier, I think we can say that as much as Lewis loved the works of Homer and was influenced by them (*The Voyage of the Dawn Treader* has been called Lewis' version of *The Odyssey*), Homer did not influence Lewis' vocation and philosophy of life. Virgil did so, and perhaps in one very specific way.

Virgil, as we have seen, was not the great originator of an epic myth. Rather, he was one who took the great myths and the work of Homer, and used that literature in new ways for his own purposes. The same could be said of C. S. Lewis. In many ways, he was not a great originator. In fact, Lewis denied originality in any of his works. He thought of himself as a translator, especially when it came to the writing of apologetics. Even in what many consider Lewis' greatest work of fiction, *Till We Have Faces*, he was re-working a myth already in existence, in this case the story of Cupid and Psyche. In this act, Lewis was modeling himself after Virgil.

Finally, did Lewis list these most influential books in order of importance? In order to answer this question, I think a few points need to be considered.

1. There is no doubt, based upon Lewis' own testimony, that he ranked George MacDonald as his number one influence.
2. If Lewis had arranged this list according to the chronological order of his own reading of these books, then the *Aeneid* certainly would have been first.
3. Lewis had a highly ordered mind, and in responding to the most trivial of questions, he was most apt to give a rather ordered and logical response.

4. There is nothing in the order of this list that suggests to me that Lewis had in mind anything other than the order of influential importance of these authors and books.

Therefore, while I am open to correction, I think that yes, Lewis listed these books in their order of importance when it came to influencing his vocation and philosophy of life.

These are just a few of the questions that have arisen for me as I have embarked upon this study of Lewis' "top ten". I am sure many more questions will be raised as we continue our journey through Lewis' reading life. However, before we close out this "interim report" I believe a few more words need to be said about Lewis' overall reading life.

We have already noted that Lewis' reading was vast. He had read most, if not all, of the greatest works in the Western canon of literature, in their original languages, by the time he was eighteen. Lewis spent the rest of his life, re-reading these great works, and adding others to the list, as well as teaching the great books.

Thus, Lewis' reading was both broad and deep. However, it was also diverse. One anecdote in closing will serve to prove the point. In an essay written about his Cambridge colleague, Richard W. Ladborough stated,

> Only about a fortnight before his death I received a card from him from Oxford: "Have been reading *Les Liaisons Dangereuses*. Wow what a book! Come to lunch on Friday (fish) and tell me about it." I'm glad to say that I went, and of course it was Jack who told *me* about it, and not the other way round.
>
> But C. S. Lewis reading *Les Liaisons Dangereuses* when on the point of death! All in all, I don't think it uncharacteristic.[430]

For those who are not familiar with the book, *Les Liaisons Dangereuses* is a French epistolary novel written by Pierre Choderlos de Lacios, published in four volumes beginning in 1782. It is the story of two aristocratic Frenchmen who are rivals and ex-lovers; they utilize seduction as a weapon to humiliate and degrade others. Many adaptations have been made of this work for the stage, film, television, radio, opera, and the ballet.

Some may ask, why would Lewis read such a book "on his deathbed" let alone at any other time? I believe he answered that question for us in his book, *Experiment in Criticism*....

> Those of us who have been true readers all our life seldom fully realize the enormous extension of our being which we owe to authors. We realize it best when we talk with an unliterary friend. He may be full of goodness and good sense but he inhabits a tiny world. In it, we should be

suffocated. The man who is contented to be only himself, and therefore less a self, is in prison. My own eyes are not enough for me, I will see through those of others. Reality, even seen through the eyes of many, is not enough. I will see what others have invented. Even the eyes of all humanity are not enough. I regret that the brutes cannot write books. Very gladly would I learn what face things present to a mouse or a bee; more gladly still would I perceive the olfactory world charged with all the information and emotion it carries for a dog.

Literary experience heals the wound, without undermining the privilege, of individuality. There are mass emotions which heal the wound; but they destroy the privilege. In them our separate selves are pooled and we sink back into sub-individuality. But in reading great literature I become a thousand men and yet remain myself. Like the night sky in the Greek poem, I see with a myriad eyes, but it is still I who see. Here, as in worship, in love, in moral action, and in knowing, I transcend myself; and am never more myself than when I do.[431]

We can thank Lewis for giving us, through his books, fresh eyes with which to see the world, and for directing us to many other great authors and books through which he enjoyed, and we can still enjoy, other sets of eyes with which to view the universe.

Acknowledgements

I am indebted to the following scholars for reading and commenting on the manuscript of this volume: Rolland Hein, Aidan Mackey, and A. T. Reyes. Without their expert advice there would be many more errors in my text than those that currently exist. It should go without saying that those errors which do remain are entirely my own responsibility.

My heartfelt gratitude goes out to the fine people of the Marion E. Wade Center at Wheaton College for once again helping me, both graciously and intelligently, with my research for this book. I count it a privilege to know Laura Schmidt, Heidi Truty, Marjorie Mead, and Chris Mitchell, the latter who was taken from us too suddenly and too soon. However, I think Chris would also remind us that our heavenly Father knows best.

Thanks too go to Roger White of Azusa Pacific University for sharing with me his research discoveries regarding C. S. Lewis' library.

I was honored and overjoyed to have The Center for the Study of C. S. Lewis & Friends at Taylor University include this volume in their C. S. Lewis & Friends Book Series. The good people of Taylor have extended their warm, Midwest hospitality to me on more than one occasion, for which I am most grateful.

My publisher, Robert Trexler, has been a source of continued encouragement to me for the past fifteen years of our acquaintance. This is the seventh book we have worked on together and, *Deo volente*, not the last.

Finally, I wish to thank my wife, Becky, for making my research and writing possible by her tireless support.

Soli Deo Gloria.

Will Vaus
Falls Church, Virginia
August 2014

ENDNOTES

1. John D. Woodbridge, *Great Leaders of the Christian Church*, Chicago: Moody Press, 1988, 355.
2. Lewis was quite conversant with the works of Freud. This is especially borne out in Armand Nicholi's excellent volume, *The Question of God*, New York: The Free Press, 2002.
3. *The Christian Century*, June 6, 1962, 719.
4. Approximately 2500 books from C. S. Lewis' library reside in the Marion E. Wade Center of Wheaton College, Wheaton, Illinois. An online link to the list of books in this collection may be viewed here: http://www.wheaton.edu/~/media/Files/Centers-and-Institutes/Wade-Center/RR-Docs/Non-archive%20Listings/Lewis_Public_shelf.pdf. An additional 150 volumes from Lewis' library reside in the Louis Round Wilson Special Collections Library of the University of North Carolina at Chapel Hill. A list of those volumes may be viewed here: http://search.lib.unc.edu/search?Ntt=%22Library+of+C.S.+Lewis%22&Ntk=Keyword&Nty=1. Perusing these lists will provide the reader with some sense of the richness of Lewis' reading life.
5. C. S. Lewis, *Reflections on the Psalms*, London: Geoffrey Bles, 1958, 1-2.
6. C. S. Lewis, *Surprised by Joy*, London: Geoffrey Bles, 1955, 12, 17.
7. Ibid, 18.
8. Ibid, 20-21.
9. Lewis, W. H. *The Lewis Papers*, Volume 3, p. 102. See also Green, Roger Lancelyn and Hooper, Walter, *C. S. Lewis: A Biography*, Glasgow: William Collins & Sons, 1980, 24.
10. *Surprised by Joy*, 40
11. Ibid, 56.
12. Ibid, 61-65.
13. Ibid, 111-112.
14. Hooper, Walter, editor, *The Collected Letters of C. S. Lewis*, Volume I, London: HarperCollins, 2000, 50-53.
15. Algernon Blackwood

Lewis' Top Ten

16 This list of authors in English is more suggestive than exhaustive. The list is based upon a reading of Lewis' letters from the period as well as what he says about his reading of the time in *Surprised by Joy*.

17 *Collected Letters*, Volume 1, 178.

18 Following Walter Hooper's dating of the C. S. Lewis letters to Arthur Greeves we may conclude that Lewis' first reading of *Phantastes* took place on 4 March 1916. Lewis said in *Surprised by Joy* that this first reading took place in October. However, as Walter Hooper pointed out to me in a personal email, Lewis was notoriously poor at dating his letters and remembering dates.

19 An Everyman edition of *Phantastes* from this time-period is still extant from Lewis' library. It is held by the Marion E. Wade Center at Wheaton College, Wheaton, Illinois. Sadly, the copy at Wheaton does not have any significant underlining or annotations by Lewis indicating his immediate reactions upon first reading the book.

20 In a letter to Professor Eliza Marian Butler, written on August 18, 1940, Lewis mentions that when he first read MacDonald he was filled with a "sense of significance" but could not have identified that significance with any one thing. Years later, when Lewis went back to re-read the same stories they became pure allegory to him. Lewis notes that the greatest pleasure in such a story takes place during the first reading when the story appears mythical but not allegorical. For this reason, when it came to the reading of his Narnia stories, Lewis did not like to have the symbols explained to children ahead of time. He thought it was much better for them just to experience the significance of the whole in its mythical quality. See Hooper, Walter, *The Collected Letters of C. S. Lewis*, Volume II, New York: HarperCollins, 2004, 438-439.

21 Lewis refers in *Surprised by Joy* to his erotic and magical perversions of the experience of Joy. By this I take Lewis to mean that as a Christian he looked back on his earlier experiences of Joy in his youth and he realized that, rather than allowing Joy to point him to God, he assumed that he could find a sense of fulfillment in erotic experience or by dabbling in magic. The older, Christian Lewis realized that these were but perversions, or rabbit trails if you will, that have the potential of distracting the seeker from the most important thing—his or

her homeward journey to the divine.
22. *Surprised by Joy*, 168-171. See also Lewis' account of his first reading of MacDonald in Lewis, C. S., *George MacDonald: An Anthology*, London: Geoffrey Bles, 1946, 20-21.
23. Lewis mentions Morris and MacDonald as influences upon his work in a letter to Charles Brady, written on October 29, 1940. See *Collected Letters*, Volume II, 629.
24. *Collected Letters*, Vol. I, 169-170.
25. Ibid, 175.
26. Ibid 176-177. Maurice Maeterlinck (1862-1949) was born in Ghent, Belgium. He was predominantly a writer of lyrical dramas. Lack of action, fatalism, mysticism, and the constant presence of death characterize the works of Maeterlinck's early period. The shadow of death looms even larger in his later plays, while his play L'Oiseau Bleu (1909) [The Blue Bird] is marked by a fairy-tale optimism. Maeterlinck developed his strongly mystical ideas in a number of prose works. In later life, Maeterlinck became known chiefly for his philosophical essays. ("Maurice Maeterlinck–Biography". Nobelprize.org. 25 Aug 2011 http://www.nobelprize.org/nobel_prizes/literature/laureates/1911/maeterlinck-bio.html)
27. *Collected Letters*, Vol. 1, 180.
28. Ibid, 206.
29. Ibid, 219.
30. Ibid, 254.
31. Ibid.
32. Ibid, 468.
33. Lewis especially enjoyed Shelley and Keats who were not Christians. However, he liked better the work of Coleridge, and even more, Wordsworth, who were more certainly Christian in their outlook.
34. See *Surprised by Joy*, pp. 202-203. Lewis also mentions meeting what he calls "mere Christianity" in a variety of authors in his Preface to Sister Penelope's translation of Athanasius. See A Religious of C. S. M. V. S. Th., *The Incarnation of the Word of God*, London: Geoffrey Bles, 1944, 8.
35. Hooper, Walter, editor, *All My Road Before Me*, San Diego: Harcourt Brace Jovanovich, 1992, 177.
36. Ibid, 362.

37 Ibid, 364. It is curious that Lewis' bookseller told him *Lilith* was out of print in 1925, because 1924 was the centenary of George MacDonald's birth and several centenary editions of his works were published including a centenary edition of *Lilith*.
38 Ibid, 412-413.
39 Ibid 18. Lewis' copy of *Lilith* at the Wade Center has several passages underlined. Perhaps the most significant is this one: "You will be dead, so long as you refuse to die." (MacDonald, George, *Lilith*, London: George Allen & Unwin Ltd., 1924, 217.) This idea haunted Lewis' mind until he began to die to himself in the years leading up to and following his return to Christian faith in 1931. Lewis came to see that Christ must do all our dying for us. (See the chapter on "The Perfect Penitent" in *Mere Christianity*.)
40 Hooper, Walter, *C. S. Lewis: Companion & Guide*, New York: HarperCollins, 1996, 801.
41 Sayer, George, *Jack: A Life of C. S. Lewis*, Wheaton: Crossway Books, 1994, 107. For other comparisons between the works of George MacDonald and C. S. Lewis see Jeff McInnis, *Shadows and Chivalry*, Hamden, CT: Winged Lion Press, 2012.
42 *Surprised by Joy*, 215
43 *The Diary of an Old Soul* is a collection of 366 daily devotional poems written by MacDonald.
44 *Collected Letters*, Volume I, 834.
45 Ibid, 835, 872. Many years later Lewis gave his copy of *The Diary of an Old Soul*, signed by George MacDonald, to Joy Davidman as a Christmas gift. The book now resides in the Marion E. Wade Collection at Wheaton College, Wheaton, Illinois. Lewis also mentions *The Diary of an Old Soul* in an undated letter to his friend Owen Barfield. See *The Collected Letters of C. S. Lewis*, Volume II, 172.
46 *Collected Letters*, Volume I, 836.
47 Ibid, 885.
48 Ibid, 901.
49 One of Greeves' copies of MacDonald, *The Seaboard Parish*, found its way into Lewis' library now preserved at the Wade Center.
50 *Surprised by Joy*, 213
51 *Collected Letters*, Volume I, 905-906.
52 Ibid, 926.
53 Ibid, 934.

54 Ibid, 935.
55 Ibid.
56 There are numerous passages underlined in Lewis' copy of *Sir Gibbie* at the Wade Center.
57 *Collected Letters*, Volume I, 936.
58 Ibid, 939.
59 Ibid, 941.
60 Ibid, 944.
61 It should be noted that G.K. Chesterton as well as many contemporary MacDonald scholars believe that his best novels contain the same seeds of imaginative genius as his fantasies and fairytales. In the scholarly journal *North Wind* #21, Adelheid Kegler considers *Wilfred Cumbermede* a "symbolist" novel and says that separating MacDonald's works between realistic and mythopoeic is "redundant." Likewise, David S. Robb, in his essay "George MacDonald's Scottish Novels" says, "While it is clear that financial necessity drove him to produce, like Scott, the number of novels he wrote, it is not inevitable that this, in turn, means that prose fiction was incapable of expressing much of what was important to him or that he was doomed to artistic failure in the medium." And also, "It has taken a long time to shift from the Lewis-derived consensus that MacDonald's novels are to be valued only for what they contain (their Christianity) rather than for what they are." (quoted in "George MacDonald: Merging Myth and Method" by Robert Trexler, *The Bulletin of the New York C.S. Lewis Society*, July-August 2003, Whole No. 396, page 4).
62 *Collected Letters*, Volume I, 949. In a letter to Arthur written on May 13, 1946, Lewis mentions how he likes the "direct preaching" in MacDonald's novels. It's the "indirect preaching" of characters like Connie in MacDonald's *Seaboard Parish* that Lewis can't stand. See *Collected Letters*, Volume II, p. 709. Lewis' statement regarding the tragedy of MacDonald being forced to write novels gives the unfortunate impression that MacDonald's novels are without literary value, something that is not entirely true.
63 Ibid, 950. Lewis underlined two significant passages in this volume. On page 453 MacDonald writes, "There is such a thing as sacred idleness, the cultivation of which is now fearfully neglected." Then, on page 477, MacDonald talks about how eternal life, immortality, apart from God is a loathsome thing.

(MacDonald, George, *What's Mine's Mine*, London: Kegan Paul, 1886.)
64　Ibid 970-971.
65　Here Lewis may be referring to Paul's teaching on predestination in Romans 9.
66　*Collected Letters*, Volume I, 975.
67　See *Collected Letters of C. S. Lewis*, Volume II, 22, 66, 92, 118-120, 124-125. See also Hooper, Walter, *The Collected Letters of C. S. Lewis*, Volume III, New York: HarperCollins, 2007, 1555.
68　See *Collected Letters*, Volume II, 43, 172, 419. See also *Collected Letters*, Volume III, 84, 118, 576, 669, 721, 806, 1011, 1264, and 1353. Lewis apparently was successful in encouraging a Mrs. Jessup to read MacDonald because MacDonald and his writings became a source of some conversation in their letters. See *Collected Letters*, Volume III, 142, 250. Mrs. Johnson also became "a convert" to MacDonald. See *Collected Letters*, Volume III, 814.
69　Lewis later attributed the similarities between his own work and that of Tolkien to common sources such as George MacDonald. See *Collected Letters*, Volume III, 1458.
70　*Collected Letters*, Volume II, 96. Lewis mentions Tolkien's shared interest in MacDonald again in a letter to Arthur Greeves on March 25, 1933 (103).
71　See, for example, *Collected Letters*, Volume III, 737, 760, 1125, 1380.
72　*Collected Letters*, Volume II, 263. Lewis was still urging Sister Penelope to read MacDonald in his letter of October 24, 1940 (451). Lewis must have been successful, in the end, in his attempt to get Sister Penelope to read MacDonald, in some fashion, for she later asked him a question about MacDonald's poetry and the source of a particular quote. See *Collected Letters*, Volume III, 123.
73　*Collected Letters*, Volume III, 174.
74　*Collected Letters*, Volume II, 376. See also Lewis' letter of April 18, 1940 to Mary Neylan (396). Lewis also recommended MacDonald's *Unspoken Sermons* in a letter to Mr. H. Morland, written on August 19, 1942 (529). In a letter to Arthur Greeves on December 10, 1942, Lewis mentions that he has introduced many people to George MacDonald in the past year, with success in most cases (539). See also Lewis' letter of May 23, 1944 to Edith Gates (616).

75 This three-volume collection is made up of sermons that MacDonald wrote but never preached to a live audience. Lewis' copies of *Unspoken Sermons* in the Wade Collection are the most heavily annotated of all Lewis' MacDonald volumes. In particular, on the endpaper of the First Series, Lewis noted various topics and the page numbers on which they appeared. Then, the Second Series of *Unspoken Sermons* contains underlining on almost every page. Many of Lewis' annotations were no doubt made in preparation for his own collection of quotes from MacDonald for his *Anthology*.

76 Lewis hoped that the publication of this anthology of George MacDonald quotes would lead to renewed publication of many of MacDonald's works that were then out of print. However, the anthology did not immediately achieve Lewis' desired result. See *Collected Letters*, Volume II, 937.

77 In selecting quotations to use for the anthology, Lewis kept a running tabulation of favorite quotes in some of his MacDonald volumes and even gave grades (α, β+, β, β-) to some of the quotes he marked for consideration. See Lewis' copy of *Annals of a Quiet Neighbourhood*, with J. Arthur Greeves' signature on the flyleaf, in the Edwin W. Brown Collection at Taylor University, Upland, Indiana.

78 Lewis, C. S., *The Screwtape Letters*, London: Geoffrey Bles, 1942, 47 (end of Letter XIII).

79 *Collected Letters*, Volume III, 246.

80 *Reflections on the Psalms*, Chapter XI, 109-119. See also Vaus, Will, *Mere Theology*, Downers Grove: InterVarsity Press, 2004, 32-41.

81 *Collected Letters*, Volume III, 245.

82 Lewis, C. S. *The Last Battle*, New York: Macmillan, 1973, Chapter XV, 161-165.

83 *George MacDonald: An Anthology*, 20.

84 *The Screwtape Letters*, 113.

85 See *Collected Letters*, Volume II, 639, letter of 20 January 1945 to Margaret Fuller and note 11. This passage is underlined in Lewis' copy of the *Unspoken Sermons*.

86 Lewis, C. S., *Mere Christianity*, London: Geoffrey Bles, 1952, 160. This passage is noted in Lewis' copy of *Donal Grant* on the endpaper of the book as well as being underlined in the text. (MacDonald, George, *Donal Grant*, London: Kegan Paul, 1883, 233.)

87 Ibid, 162.
88 Lewis, C. S. *The Great Divorce*, London: Geoffrey Bles, 1945, 113-114. See also Lewis, C. S. *The Problem of Pain*, London: Geoffrey Bles, 1940, Chapter VIII, 112-115. Significantly, Lewis underlined this bit of dialogue in *Robert Falconer*: "'Father, it will be of use in hell,' said Robert. 'God will give you no rest even there. You will have to repent some day, I do believe—if not now under the sunshine of heaven then in the torture of the awful world where there is no light but that of conscience. Would it not be better and easier to repent now?'" (MacDonald, George, *Robert Falconer*, London: Hurst & Blackett, 1868, 407.)
89 See Lewis, C. S., *Miracles*, London: Geoffrey Bles, 1947, 72, where Lewis states, as MacDonald and others did before him, "It is therefore inaccurate to define a miracle as something that breaks the laws of Nature."
90 MacDonald, George, *The Miracles of Our Lord*, London: Longmans, Green and Company, 1896, 3.
91 Ibid, 5.
92 MacDonald, George, *Dish of Orts*, London: Edwin Dalton, 1908, p. 10. Lewis thought of myth as "a real though unfocussed gleam of divine truth falling on human imagination". (See *Miracles*, 161.)
93 Ibid 316. Any reader of Lewis' fiction can attest to the fact that Lewis' invented worlds are pervaded by an atmosphere that includes a definite moral structure.
94 Ibid, 317. On numerous occasions, Lewis denied that his own fairytales were allegories.
95 Lewis, C. S., *The World's Last Night and Other Essays*, San Diego: Harcourt Brace & Company, 1987, 108-109.
96 See *Collected Letters*, Volume III, 1025, 1203, 1208, 1363.
97 Ibid, 1070.
98 Ibid, 1311-1312.
99 Sayer, 407.
100 I am indebted to the following sources for information on the life of George MacDonald: C. S. Lewis' Preface in his own *George MacDonald: An Anthology*, *Christian History & Biography* magazine's Spring 2005 issue focused on MacDonald, and Rolland Hein's masterful biography *George MacDonald: Victorian Mythmaker*.
101 Hein, Rolland, *George MacDonald: Victorian Mythmaker*,

Nashville: Star Song Publishing Group, 1993, 6.

102 MacDonald's son Ronald clarifies the nature of the influence upon his father inculcated by his Scottish religious upbringing: "Bred in a land of religious division, his whole fight was against schism.... He made no war upon the Church as he knew it—whether Independent, Presbyterian, or Anglican; his war was upon the faithlessness of the officially faithful, and, incidentally, only upon one or two Calvinistic and Augustinian dogmas exaggerated out of all proportion to their service." (Quoted in Kirstin Jeffrey Johnson's forthcoming book on MacDonald to be published by Winged Lion Press.)

103 *The Problem of Pain*, Chapter V, 65-67. See also *Mere Theology*, 62-69.

104 Hein, 30.

105 See *Mere Theology*, 165-175.

106 Again, Emeth from *The Last Battle* is an example of one who is given a second chance after death to decide for Aslan, the Christ-figure in Lewis' Narnia books. In *Mere Christianity*, Lewis states that God has not told us what his arrangements will be for those who have not heard of Christ. See *Mere Christianity*, Book II, chapter 5, 51. In *The Problem of Pain*, Lewis says that if a million chances were likely to do any good, God would give them. See *The Problem of Pain*, Chapter VIII, 112. Furthermore, all of the characters in *The Great Divorce*, who travel on the bus from hell, or purgatory, to heaven, are given a second chance, after death, to decide for God. This is the very point of Christ's descent into hell: that the souls residing there might have a second chance to respond to him. See *The Great Divorce*, 114. Regarding the redemption of animals, Lewis was clearly in agreement with MacDonald, and perhaps influenced by him. See *The Problem of Pain*, Chapter IX, 124-131.

107 *George MacDonald: An Anthology*, 13.

108 Interestingly, The Retreat was eventually rented to William Morris, another one of C. S. Lewis' favorite authors. See Hein, 307.

109 Ibid 332.

110 See *Miracles*, Appendix B, 211. See also *Collected Letters*, Volume III, letter of 23/4/51 to Dom Bede Griffiths, 111.

111 MacDonald, George, *Phantastes*, Peabody, Massachusetts: Hendrickson Publishers, 2011, 2.

112 Rolland Hein notes that *Phantastes* works upon the reader

sacramentally. (See Rolland Hein, *The Harmony Within*, Chicago: Cornerstone Press, 1999, 78.) If so, it also may work its magic not on the conscious self, but the unconscious.

113 Hein notes that the name "Anodos" is a transliteration from a Greek word that has two meanings: "having no way" and "rising". Anodos wanders through Faerie in a seemingly aimless manner, but his journey leads to his resurrection as a better person. (See *The Harmony Within*, 80.)

114 Hooper, Walter, editor, *On Stories and Other Essays on Literature*, San Diego: Harcourt Brace, 1982, 144.

115 A multiplying glass is a lens, one side of which is a plane and the other convex, but made up of a number of plane faces inclined to one another, each of which presents a separate image of the object viewed through it, so that the object is, as it were, multiplied.

116 Perhaps this part of *Phantastes* provided inspiration for Lewis to write the scene in *The Voyage of the Dawn Treader* where the invisible Dufflepuds serve King Caspian and the children from our world.

117 Perhaps from this scene in *Phantastes* Lewis got the inspiration for the scene in *The Magician's Nephew* where Digory strikes a bell in a hall of statues in the land of Charn and one of the statues comes to life.

118 Sir Aglovale de Galis is the eldest legitimate son of King Pellinore in Arthurian legend.

119 Hein notes that the woman's "song concludes that it is better to express love like a well gives water, keeping itself pure and fresh by its endless giving, than to be like a cistern, growing stagnant and impure because it only receives for itself, without outlet.... this summarizes the major theme of the entire fantasy." (*The Harmony Within*, 103)

120 *Phantastes*, 207

121 See *The Harmony Within*, 111-113.

122 *Collected Letters*, Volume I, 342.

123 It is not clear which volume of Chesterton's essays Lewis first read. Two volumes published early enough for Lewis to have read them at this time are *All Things Considered* (1908) and *Alarms and Discursions* (1910). However, the copies in Lewis' library, now at the Marion E. Wade Center in Wheaton, Illinois, are both reprints from 1924 and 1925, respectively.

124 *Surprised by Joy*, 180-181

125 Lewis was trying to support a family, the mother and daughter of a friend who died in the war. However, he could not bring himself to be truthful with his father about his relationship with the Moore family. Thus, Lewis tried to support a family on a stipend provided by his father that was fit only for a single student.

126 *All My Road Before Me*, 34-35

127 Ibid, 108

128 Ibid, 297.

129 Ibid, 296-297

130 *Surprised by Joy*, 202

131 One of Lewis' copies of *The Everlasting Man* is in the possession of Walter Hooper. The only words penned by Lewis in that copy are: "Please return to C. S. Lewis, Magdalen College, Oxford." This edition of *The Everlasting Man* is a Hodder & Stoughton reprint dated February 1927. This may indicate that Lewis did not read *The Everlasting Man* until 1927. Or perhaps, Lewis read an earlier library copy of the book, or had an earlier edition of the book in his own library that is no longer extant. It may be that the copy of *The Everlasting Man* in Hooper's possession is a copy that Lewis loaned out to others given that he often recommended this book. We simply do not know with certainty. However, based upon the existence of this 1927 edition of the book, and Lewis' own account of his reading in *Surprised by Joy*, I think we can say that Lewis probably read *The Everlasting Man* at least as early as 1927.

132 *Surprised by Joy*, 210-211.

133 *All My Road Before Me*, 395.

134 Ibid, 400.

135 Ibid, 412.

136 Ibid, 420. Lewis' copy of Chesterton's biography of Shaw (now at the Wade Center, Wheaton, Illinois) contains copious underlining, including this quote from page 186: "People have talked far too much about the paradoxes of Bernard Shaw. Perhaps his only pure paradox is this almost unconscious one; that he has tended to think that because something has satisfied generations of men it must be untrue." This is an example of what Lewis, following Owen Barfield, called chronological snobbery.

137 Or perhaps Trinity Term 1930 according to Alister McGrath's reckoning. See McGrath, Alister, *C. S. Lewis: A Life*, Carol

Stream: Tyndale, 2012.
138 *Surprised by Joy*, 221-222
139 *Collected Letters*, Volume II, 183.
140 Ibid, 198.
141 Ibid, 630.
142 *Collected Letters*, Volume III, 486.
143 Ibid, 1433.
144 *Collected Letters*, Volume II, 702-703. As Aidan Mackey has noted in "A Christian for all Christians", the influence of Chesterton's works on Lewis' return to Christian faith should not be overstated. Lewis' "intellectual and spiritual generosity" may have led him to inflate his debt to other thinkers.
145 See *Collected Letters*, Volume II, 375, 823, 941, and *Collected Letters*, Volume III, 75, 363, 652, 1353.
146 *Collected Letters*, Volume II, 824.
147 *Collected Letters*, Volume III, 703.
148 G. K. Chesterton, *The Autobiography of G. K. Chesterton*, San Francisco: Ignatius, 2006, 21.
149 Ibid, 22.
150 Maisie Ward, *Gilbert Keith Chesterton*, New York: Sheed & Ward, 1943, 4.
151 *Autobiography*, 29.
152 Sayer, *Jack: A Life of C. S. Lewis*, 22.
153 Ward, 8.
154 Ibid.
155 *Autobiography*, 191.
156 Ibid, 44. Ward, 8-9.
157 Ward, 10.
158 Ibid.
159 Ibid, 19-20.
160 *Autobiography*, 67.
161 Ward, p. 42. See also *Autobiography*, 73.
162 *Collected Letters*, Volume I, 34-35.
163 *Autobiography*, 71.
164 Ward, 43.
165 Ibid 44-45.
166 See *Surprised by Joy*, 166 ff.
167 Ward, 50, 70
168 Ibid, 70-71.
169 Ibid, 71.
170 *Christian History*, Issue 75 (Vol. XXI, No. 3), 26.

171 Ward, 45.
172 Ibid, 71-72.
173 *Christian History*, 26.
174 Ward, 159.
175 Ibid, 83.
176 Ibid, 159.
177 Ibid, 257.
178 Ibid, 117.
179 Ibid, 126.
180 Ibid, 128.
181 *Christian History*, 26.
182 Ward, 155.
183 *Collected Letters*, Volume II, 824.
184 Ward, 165.
185 Aidan Mackey has noted, "Blatchford was a declared atheist, but a man of strong principles. After he had attacked Christianity he threw *The Clarion* open to those who opposed his views, even going so far as to guarantee freedom of reply by handing over the editorship to an Anglican clergyman for a time. The articles written then were collected into a volume, 'Religious Doubts of Democracy' and Chesterton's two pieces were important." (Personal email to the author)
186 Ward, 198.
187 Ibid, 167.
188 Ibid, 367-368.
189 Ibid, 174.
190 Ibid, 252.
191 Ibid, 277.
192 Ibid, 160.
193 Lewis' copy of *Heretics* (now at the Wade Center) contains Lewis' underlining of this statement of Chesterton on pages 32 to 33: "In the case of Smith, the name is so poetical that it must be an arduous and heroic matter for the man to live up to it. The name of Smith is the name of the one trade that even kings respected, it could claim half the glory of that arma virumque which all epics acclaimed. The spirit of the smithy is so close to the spirit of song that it has mixed in a million poems, and every blacksmith is a harmonious blacksmith." Perhaps this quote suggests why Lewis named one of his characters in *The Great Divorce*, Sarah Smith of Golders Green.
194 *Collected Letters*, Volume II, 182.

195 Ibid, 171.
196 Ibid, 270-271.
197 Ibid, 177.
198 Lewis' copy of *Orthodoxy* (now at the Wade Center) contains many notations on the endpapers. Lewis especially liked Chesterton's statement on page 174 that "We want the universality that is inside all normal sentiments." This statement is very much in line with what Lewis writes in *The Abolition of Man*. Lewis also marked on page 222, "Satan fell by the force of gravity." This suggests Lewis' reason for writing *Screwtape*, that Satan can be brought down by mocking, or making fun of him. Lewis also noted this quotation on the end leaf: "The fairy tale discusses what a sane man will do in a mad world. The sober realistic novel of to-day discusses what an essential lunatic will do in a dull world." Lewis obviously agreed heartily with this statement. It is part of the reason why he wrote fairy tales. However, my favorite quote, noted by Lewis, is this one: "But perhaps God is strong enough to exult in monotony. It is possible that God says every morning, 'Do it again' to the sun…. It may be that He has the eternal appetite of infancy; for we have sinned and grown old, and our Father is younger than we."
199 *Collected Letters*, Volume II, 193.
200 Ibid, 195.
201 Ibid, 208.
202 Ibid, 212.
203 Ibid, 239.
204 Ibid.
205 Ibid, 196.
206 Ibid, 242.
207 Ibid, 250.
208 Chesterton's original title for this work was simply "What's Wrong?" It amused him, during the writing of this work, to perplex visitors to his home by setting off for his study and saying: "I must get on with What's Wrong."
209 Ward, 371.
210 Ibid, 377.
211 Ibid, 385.
212 Ibid, 373.
213 Ibid, 416.
214 Ibid, 420.

215 Ibid 439.
216 Ibid 459.
217 Ibid 468.
218 The last poem in this Chesterton collection is entitled "Who Goes Home?" which was also Lewis' original title for *The Great Divorce*. There is also a poem by Chesterton entitled "The Saracen's Head" which forms a chapter title in Lewis' *That Hideous Strength*.
219 Ward, 509.
220 Ibid 486 ff. The journal was first named *The Eye Witness*, and started in July 1911. After the Marconi affair, it was re-titled as *The New Witness*, from November 1912.
221 Ibid, 487.
222 Ibid, 509.
223 Ibid, 511.
224 Ibid, 494.
225 Ibid, 550.
226 Ibid, 578-579.
227 Ibid, 581.
228 Ibid, 565.
229 Ibid, 590.
230 Ibid, 585.
231 Ibid, 559.
232 Ibid, 633.
233 Ibid, 616.
234 Ibid, 619-620.
235 Ibid, 650-651.
236 Ibid, 652.
237 G. K. Chesterton, *The Everlasting Man*, San Francisco: Ignatius, 1993, 7.
238 Ibid, 9.
239 Ibid, 17.
240 Ibid, 23.
241 Quoted in *Mere Theology*, 67.
242 *The Everlasting Man*, 24.
243 Ibid, 26.
244 Ibid, 38.
245 http://www.britannica.com/EBchecked/topic/301721/Java-man accessed 7/23/13.
246 *The Everlasting Man*, 34.
247 Ibid, 35.

248 See *Reflections on the Psalms*, p. 115, *The Problem of Pain*, 65 ff., and *The Collected Letters of C. S. Lewis*, Volume III, 157 ff.
249 *The Everlasting Man*, 40.
250 Ibid, 42
251 Ibid.
252 Ibid, 43
253 Ibid, 50
254 Ibid, 53-55
255 Ibid, 58
256 Ibid, 61
257 Ibid, 67
258 Ibid, 78
259 Ibid, 78-79
260 Ibid, 80
261 Ibid, 84
262 Ibid, 85, 86
263 Ibid, 85
264 Ibid, 84
265 Ibid, 85
266 Ibid, 87
267 C. S. Lewis, *God in the Dock*, Grand Rapids: Eerdmans, 1970, 208-211.
268 *The Everlasting Man*, 88
269 Ibid, 95-98
270 Ibid, 99-100
271 Ibid, 93
272 Ibid, 101
273 Ibid, 113
274 Ibid, 114
275 *Collected Letters*, Volume I, 977.
276 *The Everlasting Man*, 105
277 C. S. Lewis, *Letters to Malcolm: Chiefly on Prayer*, London: Geoffrey Bles, 1964, 134.
278 *The Everlasting Man*, 109
279 Ibid, 110
280 Ibid 111
281 Ibid 116
282 Ibid 118
283 Ibid 119-121
284 Ibid 130-135
285 Ibid 142

286 Ibid 148-149
287 Ibid 149-150
288 Ibid, 159
289 Ibid
290 Ibid, 154
291 Chesterton is decidedly negative in his comments about homoeroticism in the Greek tradition. Lewis presents quite a contrast to this attitude. Neither in his letters nor in his marginalia in the works of Virgil does Lewis make any comment at all on Virgil's homoeroticism.
292 *The Everlasting Man*, 155.
293 Ibid, 157.
294 Ibid, 160.
295 Ibid, 163.
296 Ibid, 173.
297 Ibid, 170.
298 Ibid, 172.
299 Ibid, 173-174.
300 Ibid, 174.
301 Ibid, 176-177.
302 Ibid, 177-179.
303 Ibid, 181.
304 Ibid, 182.
305 Ibid, 182-184.
306 Ibid, 197.
307 Ibid, 198.
308 Ibid, 199.
309 Ibid, 200.
310 Ibid, 201.
311 Ibid, 202.
312 Ibid, 203.
313 Ibid, 211.
314 Lewis, C. S. *A Grief Observed*, London: Faber, 1961, 25.
315 *The Everlasting Man*, 213.
316 Ibid, 217.
317 Ibid, 219.
318 Ibid, 221.
319 Ibid, 222.
320 Ibid, 224-225.
321 Van A. Harvey, *A Handbook of Theological Terms*, New York: Macmillan, 1964, 28.

322 *The Everlasting Man*, 226-228.
323 Ibid, 231.
324 Ibid, 232.
325 Ibid, 233.
326 Ibid, 235.
327 Ibid, 237.
328 Ibid, 239.
329 Ibid, 241.
330 Ibid, 236.
331 Ibid, 246.
332 Ibid, 248.
333 *Surprised by Joy*, 221-222.
334 *The Everlasting Man*, 255.
335 http://www.newadvent.org/cathen/01267e.htm
336 *The Everlasting Man*, 250.
337 Ibid, 263.
338 Ibid, 270.
339 Ibid, 271.
340 Ibid, 273.
341 Ibid, 274.
342 Though Lewis does not comment on Chesterton's anti-evolutionary stance, he does discuss the sense in which Chesterton's work is dated and the sense in which it is not. See Lewis' essay entitled "Period Criticism" in Lesley Walmsley, editor, *C. S. Lewis Essay Collection*, London: HarperCollins, 2000, 79-82.
343 Lewis may very well have read Virgil for the first time earlier in his schooling. However, as far as I have been able to discover, Lewis left no record of the fact.
344 *Surprised by Joy*, 64-65. Virgil became such an important author to Lewis that it is possible he had a print of Virgil in his rooms at Magdalen College, Oxford. The print was given to his brother Warren by their Aunt Lily. See *All My Road Before Me*, 302-303.
345 See *Collected Letters*, Volume I, 79, where Lewis refers to the colossal ignorance of Virgil regarding bees as expressed in the fourth *Georgic*.
346 Ibid, 112-113.
347 Ibid, 128.
348 Ibid, 157. See also *Collected Letters*, 177. Lewis quotes Virgil often in his letters. See also *Collected Letters*, Volume II, 625,

843, 844.
349 *Collected Letters*, Vol. I, 362.
350 Ibid, 386.
351 Ibid, 419.
352 Ibid, 434.
353 Frederick Arthur Hirtzel, translator, *Virgil, Works*, London: Oxford University Press, 1900.
354 *Collected Letters*, Vol. I, 490.
355 Ibid, 935.
356 Ibid, 504.
357 Lewis' edition of the works of Virgil at UNC Chapel Hill indicates he re-read this edition on March 8th 1932, Jan 29th 1936, Aug 1942, Dec 26th 1946, Feb 22 1951, July 1952, Sept 1956, Sept 1958, and Sept 1960.
358 *Collected Letters*, Vol. II, 61, 62.
359 Ibid, 257.
360 *The Screwtape Letters*, p. 65.
361 Walter Hooper provides this translation of the quote from Virgil, *Aeneid*, Book V, 655-6. At the end of the games, the Trojan Women are tempted to burn the ships and simply stay, rather than proceed to the kingdom Aeneas has promised, "[suspended] between an unhappy love for lands now to hand and a longing for the kingdom to which the fates were calling". Lewis' own translation of these lines, given in his *Preface to Paradise Lost*, is as follows:
    ' Twixt miserable longing for the present land
    And the far realms that call them by the fates' command.
See Lewis, C. S., *A Preface to Paradise Lost*, London: Oxford University Press, 1942, 37.
362 *Collected Letters*, Volume II, 750.
363 Ibid, 754.
364 Ibid, 990-991. Tolkien must have agreed with Lewis, for he noted in his Gollancz lecture on Beowulf that the Aeneid's greatness consisted in its insistence on a long, melancholy past. See Tolkien, J. R. R., *The Monsters and the Critics*, London: George Allen & Unwin, 1983.
365 *Collected Letters*, Volume II, 723-724
366 Ibid, 918.
367 Ibid, 919.
368 *Collected Letters*, Volume III, 29, 123, 801, 957, 1021, 1117, 1348, 1624, 1641, 1644.

369 *All My Road Before Me*, 208, 234, 324, 330, 344, 346.
370 Ibid, 327.
371 Ibid, 245, 324, 392.
372 *Collected Letters*, Volume III, 111.
373 *Collected Letters*, Volume III, 416. See also *Collected Letters*, Volume III, 649, 968-969, for more comments along these lines.
374 C. S. Lewis, *English Literature in the Sixteenth Century*, London: Oxford University Press, 1954, 84.
375 *All My Road Before Me*, 84-85. The alexandrine is the leading measure in French poetry. It consists of a line of twelve syllables with major stresses on the sixth syllable (which precedes a pause) and on the last syllable, and one secondary accent in each half line.
376 C. S. Lewis, *The Pilgrim's Regress*, London: Sheed & Ward, 1935, p. 137.
377 *Collected Letters*, Volume III, 1526.
378 *Collected Letters*, Volume II, 156.
379 *The Problem of Pain*, 6-7.
380 A. T. Reyes, *C. S. Lewis' lost Aeneid*, New Haven: Yale University Press, 2011, 4.
381 Ibid, 4-5
382 C. S. Lewis, *Arthurian Torso*, London: Oxford University Press, 1948, 184.
383 *Collected Letters*, Volume III, 1034.
384 C. S. Lewis, *The Discarded Image*, Cambridge: Cambridge University Press, 1964, 86.
385 The bit of translation of the *Aeneid* that appears in *The Discarded Image* may have first been written by Lewis for his much earlier lectures upon which *The Discarded Image* was based. Thus, we do not know with certainty whether or not Lewis was continuing to work on his translation of the Aeneid in the 1960s.
386 Reyes, 2
387 *Collected Letters*, Volume III, 1540-1541.
388 Ibid, 307-308.
389 In 1922 Lewis wrote some notes on Virgil's life and an introduction to the *Aeneid* for his "adopted sister" Maureen Moore, with whom he read the *Aeneid*. See *All My Road Before Me*, 109, 110, 117, 121, 123-124, 126, 153. As far as I know, these notes are no longer extant.
390 See also Lewis' comments on Virgil in his essay entitled "Historicism" in *Fern-seed and Elephants*, Glasgow: Collins,

1977, 49-50.
391 *A Preface to Paradise Lost*, 32.
392 Ibid, 33-34
393 Ibid, 35-36
394 Ibid, 37
395 *Collected Letters*, Volume II, 77-78.
396 *Collected Letters*, Volume III, 1082.
397 This brief biography is based in part upon the biographical note in James Rhoades' translation of *The Poems of Virgil*, Chicago: University of Chicago Press, 1952, v-vi.
398 A *Life of Virgil* attributed to Suetonius (a Roman historian born in 70 CE), survives in a fourth century commentary by Aelius Donatus, a Roman grammarian and teacher of rhetoric. See http://www.fordham.edu/halsall/pwh/suet-vergil.asp. Everything that Donatus writes is traditional and therefore may or may not have anything really to do with the actuality of Virgil's life. The tradition may well have passed from Suetonius to Donatus, and may be correct. However, at present, we have no way of verifying the accuracy of the traditional statements about the life of Virgil. I present here what we know from Donatus with the notation that we should take much of what he says with a grain of salt.
399 http://www.fordham.edu/halsall/pwh/suet-vergil.asp
400 Ibid.
401 The toga virilis was a white toga assumed by boys at the age of fifteen, symbolizing manhood and citizenship. Coincidentally, the Epicurean poet Lucretius died on the same day, Virgil's fifteenth birthday.
402 http://www.fordham.edu/halsall/pwh/suet-vergil.asp
403 Donatus says this is because at this time Virgil spoke very slowly, almost like an uneducated man.
404 http://www.fordham.edu/halsall/pwh/suet-vergil.asp
405 Ibid.
406 Rhoades, vi
407 Lecture by Susanna Braund, *Introduction to Virgil and the Aeneid*, https://itunes.apple.com/us/itunes-u/virgils-aeneid/id384233916?mt=10
408 Rhoades, vi.
409 http://www.fordham.edu/halsall/pwh/suet-vergil.asp
410 Rhoades, v.
411 Ibid, vi.

412 http://www.fordham.edu/halsall/pwh/suet-vergil.asp
413 Braund, *Introduction to Virgil and the Aeneid*, lecture at Stanford University.
414 http://www.fordham.edu/halsall/pwh/suet-vergil.asp
415 Ibid.
416 Rhoades, vi.
417 Braund.
418 http://www.fordham.edu/halsall/pwh/suet-vergil.asp
419 Rhoades, vi.
420 http://www.fordham.edu/halsall/pwh/suet-vergil.asp
421 Rhoades, vi. Beside the *Eclogues, Georgics,* and *The Aeneid*, the works ascribed to Virgil are likely not by him. These fall under what is called the Appendix Vergiliana. These works may contain certain elements that were actually written by Virgil (such as his epitaph), but it is impossible to be certain which items in the Appendix are authentic.
422 http://www.fordham.edu/halsall/pwh/suet-vergil.asp
423 Ibid.
424 Braund, Lecture I.
425 Reyes, 1.
426 *Reflections on the Psalms*, 101, 108.
427 This summary is adapted from the following source: http://www.shmoop.com/aeneid/summary.html. The book titles are taken from Fitzgerald's translation of *The Aeneid*. See Fitzgerald, Robert, translator, *The Aeneid*, New York: Vintage Books, 1990.
428 *The Incarnation of the Word of God*, 6-7.
429 See Will Vaus, *The Hidden Story of Narnia*, Hamden, CT: Winged Lion Press, 2010.
430 James T. Como, editor, *C. S. Lewis at the Breakfast Table*, San Diego: Harcourt Brace Jovanovich, 1992, 104.
431 C. S. Lewis, *An Experiment in Criticism*, New York: Cambridge University Press, 1983, 140-141.

BIBLIOGRAPHY

A Religious of C. S. M. V., St. Th., *The Incarnation of the Word of God*, London: Geoffrey Bles, 1944.

Camps, W. A., *An Introduction to Virgil's Aeneid*, London: Oxford University Press, 1969.

Como, James T., editor, *C. S. Lewis at the Breakfast Table*, San Diego: Harcourt Brace Jovanovich, 1992.

Chesterton, G. K., *The Collected Poems of G. K. Chesterton*, New York: Dodd, Mead & Company, 1932.

_____, *Orthodoxy*, Wheaton: Harold Shaw, 1994.

_____, *The Autobiography of G. K. Chesterton*, San Francisco: Ignatius, 2006.

_____, *The Everlasting Man*, San Francisco: Ignatius, 1993.

Fitzgerald, Robert, translator, *The Aeneid*, New York: Vintage Books, 1990.

Green, Roger Lancelyn and Hooper, Walter, *C. S. Lewis: A Biography*, Glasgow: William Collins & Sons, 1980.

Harvey, Van A. *A Handbook of Theological Terms*, New York: Macmillan, 1964.

Hein, Rolland, *George MacDonald: Victorian Mythmaker*, Nashville: Star Song Publishing Group, 1993.

_____, *The Harmony Within: The Spiritual Vision of George MacDonald*, Chicago: Cornerstone Press, 1999.

Hooper, Walter, editor, *All My Road Before Me*, San Diego: Harcourt Brace Jovanovich, 1992.

_____, *C. S. Lewis: Companion & Guide*, New York: HarperCollins, 1996.

_____, editor, *Fern-seed and Elephants*, Glasgow: Collins, 1977.

_____, editor, *On Stories and Other Essays on Literature*, San Diego: Harcourt Brace, 1982.

_____, editor, *The Collected Letters of C. S. Lewis*, Volumes I-III, London: HarperCollins, 2000, 2004, 2007.

Lewis, C. Day, *The Aeneid of Virgil*, London: Oxford University Press, 1952.

Lewis' Top Ten

Lewis, C. S. *A Grief Observed*, London: Faber, 1961.

____, *A Preface to Paradise Lost*, London: Oxford University Press, 1942.

____, *An Experiment in Criticism*, New York: Cambridge University Press, 1983.

____, *Arthurian Torso*, London: Oxford University Press, 1948.

____, *English Literature in the Sixteenth Century*, London: Oxford University Press, 1954.

____, *George MacDonald: An Anthology*, London: Geoffrey Bles, 1946.

____, *God in the Dock*, Grand Rapids: Eerdmans, 1970.

____, *Letters to Malcolm: Chiefly on Prayer*, London: Geoffrey Bles, 1964.

____, *Mere Christianity*, London: Geoffrey Bles, 1952.

____, *Miracles*, London: Geoffrey Bles, 1947.

____, *Reflections on the Psalms*, London: Geoffrey Bles, 1958.

____, *Surprised by Joy*, London: Geoffrey Bles, 1955.

____, *The Discarded Image*, Cambridge: Cambridge University Press, 1964.

____, *The Great Divorce*, London: Geoffrey Bles, 1945.

____, *The Last Battle*, New York: Macmillan, 1973.

____, *The Pilgrim's Regress*, London: Sheed & Ward, 1935.

____, *The Problem of Pain*, London: Geoffrey Bles, 1940.

____, *The Screwtape Letters*, London: Geoffrey Bles, 1942.

____, *The World's Last Night and Other Essays*, San Diego: Harcourt Brace & Company, 1987.

MacDonald, George, *Dish of Orts*, London: Edwin Dalton, 1908.

____, *Donal Grant*, London: Kegan Paul, 1883.

____, *Lilith*, London: George Allen & Unwin Ltd., 1924.

____, *Phantastes*, Peabody, Massachusetts: Hendrickson Publishers, 2011.

____, *Robert Falconer*, London: Hurst & Blackett, 1868.

____, *The Miracles of Our Lord*, London: Longmans, Green and Company, 1896.

____, *What's Mine's Mine*, London: Kegan Paul, 1886.

MacDonald, Michael H. & Tadie, Andrew A., *The Riddle of Joy: G. K. Chesterton & C. S. Lewis*, Grand Rapids: Eerdmans, 1989.

McGrath, Alister, *C. S. Lewis: A Life*, Carol Stream: Tyndale, 2012.

McInnes, Jeff, *Shadows and Chivalry*, Hamden, CT: Winged Lion Press, 2012.

Nicholi, Armand, *The Question of God*, New York: The Free Press, 2002.

Reyes, A. T. *C. S. Lewis' lost Aeneid*, New Haven: Yale University Press, 2011.

Rhoades, James, translator, *The Poems of Virgil*, Chicago: University of Chicago Press, 1952.

Sayer, George, *Jack: A Life of C. S. Lewis*, Wheaton: Crossway Books, 1994.

Vaus, Will, *Mere Theology*, Downers Grove: InterVarsity Press, 2004.

____, *The Hidden Story of Narnia*, Hamden, CT: Winged Lion Press, 2010.

Walmsley, Lesley, editor, *C. S. Lewis Essay Collection*, London: HarperCollins, 2000.

Ward, Maisie, *Gilbert Keith Chesterton*, New York: Sheed & Ward, 1943.

Woodbridge, John D., *Great Leaders of the Christian Church*, Chicago: Moody Press, 1988.

INDEX

A
Aeschylus, 6, 11
Anglicanism, 15, 23, 47, 49, 51, 52
Aquinas, Thomas, 52, 57
Arcadians, 68, 111-113, 116, 118
Arianism, 73, 76
Art, 18, 48, 53, 59, 61, 82, 83-84, 121
Athanasius, 73, 125
Atheism, 11, 45, 49, 81
Augustus, 88, 89, 90, 91, 94, 108, 113

B
Bacchus, 5, 110
Balfour, Arthur James, 3, 51-52, 125
Barfield, Owen, 12, 15, 84
Baring, Maurice, 53, 55
BBC, 46, 57
Belloc, Hilaire, 49, 56, 57
Blatchford, Robert, 50
Boethius, 3, 123
Boswell, James, 3, 6, 76, 125
Browning, Robert, 45, 46, 48, 49, 50
Buddhism, 62, 64, 65, 68, 74
Byron, Lady, 22-23

C
Calvinism, 20-21
Camilla, 83, 111, 119
Carroll, Lewis, 23
Carthage, 64-66, 93-95, 101-103
Catholicism, 23, 24, 49, 53, 54, 55, 56, 57, 64, 68, 72, 74, 76
Catullus, 6, 88
Caves, 28, 29, 35, 59, 67, 68, 102, 106, 112
Chesterton, Cecil, 47, 54, 55, 56
Chesterton, G. K., 3, 11, 12, 45-78, 84, 125
  Works by,
  The Ballad of the White Horse, 46, 53
  Orthodoxy, 52, 53, 57
  Conversion, 49
Christ, 16, 18, 22, 23, 24, 25, 49, 50, 58, 62, 63, 64, 67, 68, 72, 91-92, 125
  Divinity, 69-71
Christmas, 67-69, 72
Coleridge, Samuel Taylor, 6, 52
Confucianism, 61, 62, 64, 68
Creed, 63, 72, 73

D
Dance, 34, 35, 112
Dante, 17, 86, 91
Darwin, Charles, 21, 60, 76, 77
Death, 5, 12, 13, 14, 15, 17, 19, 22, 23, 24, 25, 33, 39, 41, 42, 47, 57, 76, 87, 88, 89, 91, 103, 106, 107, 108, 114, 115, 116, 117, 118, 119, 121, 127
Demons, 63-65, 70, 81

Demosthenes, 6, 82
Dickens, Charles, 52, 53
Donatus, 87, 88, 89, 90
Dreams, 11, 13, 26, 27, 30, 32, 34, 35, 36, 40, 46, 48, 50, 59, 62, 63, 66, 75, 86, 87, 94, 97, 103, 104, 108, 109, 110
Dyson, H. V. D., 14, 63

E
Education, 4-6, 20-21, 47-9, 81, 83, 87, 88, 91
Elysium, 105, 108
Erotic, 9, 66
Etruscans, 115-117
Euripides, 5, 6
Evolution, 21, 59, 60, 62, 72, 77, 78

F
Fairy tales, 10, 11, 14, 15, 18, 20, 24, 26-42, 47, 53, 63, 75
Father Brown, 51, 53, 55, 56, 57
Francis of Assisi, 46, 55
Friendship, 9, 10, 12, 14, 15, 19, 22, 23, 41, 42, 46, 48, 49, 51, 53, 55, 57, 58, 63, 82, 88-89, 91, 94, 106, 119
Furies, the, 109-110, 122

G
Golden bough, 106-108
Greeves, Arthur, 9, 10, 12, 13, 14, 15, 26
Grief, 24, 94, 114, 117, 118, 121
Griffiths, Dom Bede, 46, 83, 84

H
Harpies, the, 100, 109-110
Heaven, 11, 26, 58, 64, 66, 67, 69, 71, 72, 77, 84, 92, 105, 115, 117, 119
Helen of Troy, 95, 98, 107
Hell, 3, 10, 17, 22, 73, 83, 108
Herbert, George, 3, 11, 12, 125
Homeliness, 12
Homer, 3, 6, 66, 81, 82, 85-86, 90, 95, 98, 101, 109, 111, 126
  The Iliad, 6, 61, 82, 90, 91, 95, 98, 111
  The Odyssey, 90, 101, 109, 126
Homoeroticism, 66
Homosexuality, 88, 104, 114, 127
Horace, 5, 48, 89

I
Imagination, 5, 6, 9, 18, 25, 46, 63, 69, 125
Islam, 62, 71, 74, 76

J
James, Henry & William, 54
Jesus, 3, 16, 58, 67-69, 71, 72, 77
Johnson, Samuel, 3, 11, 76
Judaism, 62, 71, 72, 75
Jupiter, 68, 94, 102, 105, 110, 113, 115-117, 120-122

K
Keats, John, 6, 14

Kirkpatrick, William, 6, 81

L
Latins, 110-111, 118-122
Les Liaisons Dangereuses, 127
Lewis, C. S.
  Books by,
  A Grief Observed, 24, 72
  Dymer, 12, 13, 86
  English Literature in the Sixteenth Century, 84
  Experiment in Criticism, 127-8
  George MacDonald: An Anthology, 15, 16, 18, 22
  Letters to Malcolm, 63
  Mere Christianity, 17, 21, 72, 125
  Miracles, 17, 24
  Perelandra, 27
  Prince Caspian, 121
  Reflections on the Psalms, 4, 16, 91
  Surprised by Joy, 9, 11, 46, 75, 81
  The Great Divorce, 17, 66, 77
  The Last Battle, 16, 108
  The Lion, the Witch and the Wardrobe, 121
  The Magician's Nephew, 27
  The Pilgrim's Regress, 30, 58, 77, 84
  The Problem of Pain, 21, 78, 85
  The Screwtape Letters, 10, 16, 77, 83
  The Silver Chair, 41, 106, 108
  The Voyage of the Dawn Treader, 40, 101, 126
  The World's Last Night, 18
  Till We Have Faces, 75, 77, 126
  Conversion to theism, 12
  Trilemma, 70
Lewis, W. H., 5, 6, 15
Love, 20, 24, 28, 34, 37, 38, 39, 42, 49, 66, 73, 93, 94, 95, 96, 100, 102, 104, 114, 119, 120, 127, 128
Lucretius, 6, 88

M
MacDonald, George, 3, 8, 9-42, 45, 46, 47, 125, 126
  Books by,
  At the Back of the North Wind, 10, 24
  The Diary of an Old Soul, 12, 14, 24
  Dish of Orts, 18, 25
  Lilith, 11, 12, 13, 14, 25
  Sir Gibbie, 10, 13, 14, 24
  The Miracles of Our Lord, 17, 24
  The Princess and Curdie, 13, 25
  The Princess and the Goblin, 13, 24, 47
  Unspoken Sermons, 15, 17, 19, 23
  Wilfrid Cumbermede, 13-14
Magic, 9, 32, 34, 45, 63, 105, 116, 121
Malory, Thomas, 6, 9
Manichaeism, 73, 76
Marcellus, 90, 108
Mary, Blessed Virgin, 67-68, 91-92

Milton, John, 5, 6, 48, 86
   Paradise Lost, 5, 85
Miracles, 17, 24, 70
Monotheism, 62, 64
Morris, William, 6, 9, 15, 46, 48
Music, 9, 16, 17, 27, 28, 29, 31, 34, 35, 36, 37, 38, 39, 40, 41, 55, 77, 96, 108, 110, 112
Myth, 5, 6, 9, 11, 50, 58, 62, 63, 65, 66, 67, 68, 70, 73, 74, 75, 76, 77, 90, 92, 106, 112, 126

N
Narnia, 3, 11, 15, 30, 58, 77, 101, 108, 126
Newman, John Henry, 52, 53
Neylan, Mary, 15-16
Novalis, 20, 21, 26
Nymphs, 93, 116, 120

O
O'Connor, John, 51
Originality, 82, 124
Otto, Rudolf, 3, 125

P
Paganism, 46, 50, 61, 62, 63, 64, 65, 67, 73, 74, 75, 81, 92
Plato, 11, 64, 68, 76, 92, 125
Polytheism, 62, 64, 76
Pius XI, Pope, 56, 57
Prayer, 16, 21, 31, 57, 63, 81, 103, 104, 114
Preaching, 14, 21, 22, 47, 51, 71
Proserpina, 106, 108

Pygmalion, 28, 94

R
Reason, 63
Romantics, 11, 20
Rome, 15, 56, 57, 65-67, 83, 87-91, 93-94, 108, 109, 112
Rutulians, 94, 110-112, 114-117, 120-121

S
Sayers, Dorothy, 56, 83
Science, 20, 59, 60, 78
Scott, Walter, 6, 76
Second Coming, 18
Sex, 64
Shadow, 9, 27, 28, 30, 31, 32, 35, 39, 40, 42
Shaw, George Bernard, 11, 46, 49, 52, 53, 56
Sibyl, the, 92, 101, 106-108
Sister Penelope, 15, 125
Sophocles, 6, 84

T
Tacitus, 6, 89
Tartarus, 105, 108
Tennyson, 48, 49
The Apostle Paul, 3, 15, 73
The Bible, 3, 16, 21, 25, 84
The Christian Century, 3, 4, 126
The Gospel of Matthew, 71, 72, 77
Tolkien, J. R. R., 14, 15, 63, 83, 85
Tolstoy, Leo, 49, 84
Trinity, the, 60, 73
Twain, Mark, 5, 24

U

Underworld, 83, 105, 106-108, 122
Ulysses/Odysseus, 96, 97, 101, 107

V

Virgil, 3, 5, 6, 11, 17, 62, 66, 81-122, 126, 127
    Books by,
        Eclogues, 83, 87-89, 91
        Georgics, 83, 87, 89, 90
Vocation, 3, 6, 83, 86, 126, 127
Voltaire, 11, 76, 77

W

War, 45, 49, 51, 54, 61, 65, 73, 75, 82, 87, 88, 89, 93, 94, 95, 96, 97, 98, 99, 103, 104, 105, 106, 107, 110, 111, 112, 113, 114, 116, 118, 119, 120
Ward, Maisie, 51, 53
Wells, H. G., 5, 11, 54, 58, 60, 77
Williams, Charles, 3, 46, 84, 85, 125
Wordsworth, William, 3, 11, 125
    The Prelude, 3, 84

Y

Yeats, William Butler, 6, 45

About the Author

Will Vaus

- was born in Sleepy Hollow, New York and grew up in La Jolla, California.
- is the son of Jim Vaus, former organized crime wiretapper who came to Christ through the ministry of Billy Graham in 1949.
- holds a Bachelor of Arts degree in drama from the University of California at San Diego and a Master of Divinity degree from Princeton Theological Seminary.
- has served as a pastor in California, South Carolina, Pennsylvania, and West Virginia.
- is the president of Will Vaus Ministries, through which he has communicated the love of Christ around the world since 1988.
- is the author of *Mere Theology: A Guide to the Thought of C.S. Lewis*, *My Father Was a Gangster: The Jim Vaus Story*, *The Professor of Narnia: The C.S. Lewis Story*, *Speaking of Jack: A C.S. Lewis Discussion Guide*, *The Hidden Story of Narnia: A Book-by-Book Guide to Lewis' Spiritual Themes*, *Keys To Growth: Meditations on the Acts of the Apostles*, *Open Before Christmas: Devotional Thoughts for the Holiday Season*, *God's Love Letter: Reflections on I John*, and *Sheldon Vanauken: The Man Who Received a Severe Mercy*.
- and his wife, Becky, have been married since 1988 and have three sons: James, Jonathan and Joshua.
- has a website you can visit: www.willvaus.com

Other Books of Interest

C. S. Lewis

C. S. Lewis: Views From Wake Forest - Essays on C. S. Lewis
Michael Travers, editor

Contains sixteen scholarly presentations from the international C. S. Lewis convention in Wake Forest, NC. Walter Hooper shares his important essay "Editing C. S. Lewis," a chronicle of publishing decisions after Lewis' death in 1963.

"*Scholars from a variety of disciplines address a wide range of issues. The happy result is a fresh and expansive view of an author who well deserves this kind of thoughtful attention.*"
      Diana Pavlac Glyer, author of *The Company They Keep*

The Hidden Story of Narnia:
A Book-By-Book Guide to Lewis' Spiritual Themes
Will Vaus

A book of insightful commentary equally suited for teens or adults – Will Vaus points out connections between the *Narnia* books and spiritual/biblical themes, as well as between ideas in the *Narnia* books and C. S. Lewis' other books. Learn what Lewis himself said about the overarching and unifying thematic structure of the Narnia books. That is what this book explores; what C. S. Lewis called "the hidden story" of Narnia. Each chapter includes questions for individual use or small group discussion.

Why I Believe in Narnia:
33 Reviews and Essays on the Life and Work of C.S. Lewis
James Como

Chapters range from reviews of critical books , documentaries and movies to evaluations of Lewis' books to biographical analysis.
"*A valuable , wide-ranging collection of essays by one of the best informed and most accute commentators on Lewis' work and ideas.*"
      Peter Schakel, author of *Imagination & the Arts in C.S. Lewis*

C. S. Lewis Goes to Heaven: A Reader's Guide to The Great Divorce
David G. Clark

This is the first book devoted solely to this often neglected book and the first to reveal several important secrets Lewis concealed within the story. Lewis felt his imaginary trip to Hell and Heaven was far better than his book *The Screwtape Letters*, which has become a classic. Clark has taught courses on Lewis for more than 30 years and is a New Testament and Greek scholar with a Doctor of Philosophy degree in Biblical Studies. Readers will discover the many literary and biblical influences Lewis utilized in writing his brilliant novel.

C. S. Lewis & Philosophy as a Way of Life: His Philosophical Thoughts
Adam Barkman

C. S. Lewis is rarely thought of as a "philosopher" per se despite having both studied and taught philosophy for several years at Oxford. Lewis's long journey to Christianity was essentially philosophical – passing through seven different stages. This 624 page book is an invaluable reference for C. S. Lewis scholars and fans alike

C. S. Lewis: His Literary Achievement
Colin Manlove

"This is a positively brilliant book, written with splendor, elegance, profundity and evidencing an enormous amount of learning. This is probably not a book to give a first-time reader of Lewis. But for those who are more broadly read in the Lewis corpus this book is an absolute gold mine of information. The author gives us a magnificent overview of Lewis' many writings, tracing for us thoughts and ideas which recur throughout, and at the same time telling us how each book differs from the others. I think it is not extravagant to call C. S. Lewis: His Literary Achievement a tour de force."
  Robert Merchant, *St. Austin Review*, Book Review Editor

Mythopoeic Narnia: Memory, Metaphor, and Metamorphoses in C. S. Lewis's The Chronicles of Narnia
Salwa Khoddam

Dr. Khoddam offers a fresh approach to the *Narnia* books based on an inquiry into Lewis' readings and use of classical and Christian symbols. She explores the literary and intellectual contexts of these stories, the traditional myths and motifs, and places them in the company of the greatest Christian mythopoeic works of Western Literature. In Lewis' imagination, memory and metaphor interact to advance his purpose – a Christian metamorphosis. *Mythopoeic Narnia* opens the door for readers into the magical world of the Western imagination.

Speaking of Jack: A C. S. Lewis Discussion Guide
Will Vaus

C. S. Lewis Societies have been forming around the world since the first one started in New York City in 1969. Will Vaus has started and led three groups himself. *Speaking of Jack* is the result of Vaus' experience in leading those Lewis Societies. Included here are introductions to most of Lewis' books as well as questions designed to stimulate discussion about Lewis' life and work. These materials have been "road-tested" with real groups made up of young and old, some very familiar with Lewis and some newcomers. *Speaking of Jack* may be used in an existing book discussion group, to start a C. S. Lewis Society, or as a guide to your own exploration of Lewis' books.

Light: C.S. Lewis's First and Final Short Story
Charlie W. Starr

"As literary journalism, both investigative and critical, it is top shelf"
  James Como, author of *Remembering C.S. Lewis*

"Starr shines a new and illuminating light on one of Lewis's most intriguing stories"
  Michael Ward, author of *Planet Narnia*

GEORGE MACDONALD

Diary of an Old Soul & The White Page Poems
George MacDonald and Betty Aberlin

The first edition of George MacDonald's book of daily poems included a blank page opposite each page of poems. Readers were invited to write their own reflections on the "white page." MacDonald wrote: "Let your white page be ground, my print be seed, growing to golden ears, that faith and hope may feed." Betty Aberlin responded to MacDonald's invitation with daily poems of her own.

Betty Aberlin's close readings of George MacDonald's verses and her thoughtful responses to them speak clearly of her poetic gifts and spiritual intelligence.
    Luci Shaw, poet

George MacDonald: Literary Heritage and Heirs
Roderick McGillis, editor

This latest collection of 14 essays sets a new standard that will influence MacDonald studies for many more years. George MacDonald experts are increasingly evaluating his entire corpus within the nineteenth century context.

This comprehensive collection represents the best of contemporary scholarship on George MacDonald.
    Rolland Hein, author of *George MacDonald: Victorian Mythmaker*

In the Near Loss of Everything: George MacDonald's Son in America
Dale Wayne Slusser

In the summer of 1887, George MacDonald's son Ronald, newly engaged to artist Louise Blandy, sailed from England to America to teach school. The next summer he returned to England to marry Louise and bring her back to America. On August 27, 1890, Louise died leaving him with an infant daughter. Ronald once described losing a beloved spouse as "the near loss of everything". Dale Wayne Slusser unfolds this poignant story with unpublished letters and photos that give readers a glimpse into the close-knit MacDonald family. Also included is Ronald's essay about his father, *George MacDonald: A Personal Note*, plus a selection from Ronald's 1922 fable, *The Laughing Elf*, about the necessity of both sorrow and joy in life.

A Novel Pulpit: Sermons From George MacDonald's Fiction
David L. Neuhouser

Each of the sermons has an introduction giving some explanation of the setting of the sermon or of the plot, if that is necessary for understanding the sermon. *"MacDonald's novels are both stimulating and thought-provoking. This collection of sermons from ten novels serve to bring out the 'freshness and brilliance' of MacDonald's message." from the author's introduction*

Behind the Back of the North Wind: Essays on George MacDonald's Classic Book
Edited and with Introduction by John Pennington and Roderick McGillis

The unique blend of fairy tale atmosphere and social realism in this novel laid the groundwork for modern fantasy literature. Sixteen essays by various authors are accompanied by an instructive introduction, extensive index, and beautiful illustrations.

Through the Year with George MacDonald: 366 Daily Readings
Rolland Hein, editor

These page-length excerpts from sermons, novels and letters are given an appropriate theme/heading and a complementary Scripture passage for daily reading. An inspiring introduction to the artistic soul and Christian vision of George MacDonald.

Shadows and Chivalry:
C.S. Lewis and George MacDonald on Suffering, Evil, and Death
Jeff McInnis

Shadows and Chivalry studies the influence of George MacDonald, a nineteenth-century Scottish novelist and fantasy writer, upon one of the most influential writers of modern times, C. S. Lewis—the creator of Narnia, literary critic, and best-selling apologist. This study attempts to trace the overall affect of MacDonald's work on Lewis's thought and imagination. Without ever ceasing to be a story of one man's influence upon another, the study also serves as an exploration of each writer's thought on, and literary visions of, good and evil.

POETS AND POETRY

In the Eye of the Beholder: How to See the World Like a Romantic Poet
Louis Markos

Born out of the French Revolution and its radical faith that a nation could be shaped and altered by the dreams and visions of its people, British Romantic Poetry was founded on a belief that the objects and realities of our world, whether natural or human, are not fixed in stone but can be molded and transformed by the visionary eye of the poet. A separate bibliographical essay is provided for readers listing accessible biographies of each poet and critical studies of their work.

The Cat on the Catamaran: A Christmas Tale
John Martin

Here is a modern-day parable of a modern-day cat with modern-day attitudes. Riverboat Dan is a "cool" cat on a perpetual vacation from responsibility. He's *The Cat on the Catamaran* – sailing down the river of life. Dan keeps his guilty conscience from interfering with his fun until he runs into trouble. But will he have the courage to believe that it's never too late to change course? (For ages 10 to adult)

The Half Blood Poems
Inspired by the Stories of J.K. Rowling
Christine Lowther

Like Harry Potter, Christine's poetry can soar above the tragic to discover the heroic and beautiful. There are 71 poems divided into seven chapters that correspond to the seven books. Fans of Harry Potter will experience once again many of the emotions they felt reading the books – emotions presented most effectively through a poet's words.

Pop Culture

To Love Another Person: A Spiritual Journey Through Les Miserables
John Morrison

The powerful story of Jean Valjean's redemption is beloved by readers and theater goers everywhere. In this companion and guide to Victor Hugo's masterpiece, author John Morrison unfolds the spiritual depth and breadth of this classic novel and broadway musical.

Through Common Things: Philosophical Reflections on Popular Culture
Adam Barkman

"Barkman presents us with an amazingly wide-ranging collection of philosophical reflections grounded in the everyday things of popular culture – past and present, eastern and western, factual and fictional. Throughout his encounters with often surprising subject-matter (the value of darkness?), he writes clearly and concisely, moving seamlessly between Aristotle and anime, Lord Buddha and Lord Voldemort.... This is an informative and entertaining book to read!"
     Doug Bloomberg, Professor of Philosophy, Institute for Christian Studies

Spotlight:
A Close-up Look at the Artistry and Meaning of Stephenie Meyer's Twilight Novels
John Granger

Stephenie Meyer's *Twilight* saga has taken the world by storm. But is there more to *Twilight* than a love story for teen girls crossed with a cheesy vampire-werewolf drama? *Spotlight* reveals the literary backdrop, themes, artistry, and meaning of the four Bella Swan adventures. *Spotlight* is the perfect gift for serious *Twilight* readers.

Virtuous Worlds: The Video Gamer's Guide to Spiritual Truth
John Stanifer

Popular titles like *Halo 3* and *The Legend of Zelda: Twilight Princess* fly off shelves at a mind-blowing rate. John Stanifer, an avid gamer, shows readers specific parallels between Christian faith and the content of their favorite games. Written with wry humor (including a heckler who frequently pokes fun at the author) this book will appeal to gamers and non-gamers alike. Those unfamiliar with video games may be pleasantly surprised to find that many elements in those "virtual worlds" also qualify them as "virtuous worlds."

The Many Faces of Katniss Everdeen: Exploring the Heroine of The Hunger Games
Valerie Estelle Frankel

Katniss is the heroine who's changed the world. Like Harry Potter, she explodes across genres: She is a dystopian heroine, a warrior woman, a reality TV star, a rebellious adolescent. She's surrounded by the figures of Roman history, from Caesar and Cato to Cinna and Coriolanus Snow. She's also traveling the classic heroine's journey. As a child soldier, she faces trauma; as a growing teen, she battles through love triangles and the struggle to be good in a harsh world. This book explores all this and more, while taking a look at the series' symbolism, from food to storytelling, to show how Katniss becomes the greatest power of Panem, the girl on fire.

Myths and Motifs of The Mortal Instruments
Valerie Estelle Frankel

With vampires, fairies, angels, romance, steampunk, and modern New York all in one series of books, Cassandra Clare is exploding onto the scene. This book explores the deeper world of the Shadowhunters. There's something for everyone, as this book reveals unseen lore within the bestselling series.

BIOGRAPHY

Sheldon Vanauken: The Man Who Received "A Severe Mercy"
Will Vaus

In this biography we discover: Vanauken the struggling student, the bon-vivant lover, the sailor who witnessed the bombing of Pearl Harbor, the seeker who returned to faith through C. S. Lewis, the beloved professor of English literature and history, the feminist and anti-war activist who participated in the March on the Pentagon, the bestselling author, and Vanauken the convert to Catholicism. What emerges is the portrait of a man relentlessly in search of beauty, love, and truth, a man who believed that, in the end, he found all three.

"This is a charming biography about a doubly charming man who wrote a triply charming book. It is a great way to meet the man behind A Severe Mercy."
      Peter Kreeft, author of *Jacob's Ladder: 10 Steps to Truth*

Remembering Roy Campbell: The Memoirs of his Daughters, Anna and Tess
Introduction by Judith Lütge Coullie, Editor
Preface by Joseph Pearce

Anna and Teresa Campbell were the daughters of the handsome young South African poet and writer, Roy Campbell (1901-1957), and his beautiful English wife, Mary Garman. In their frank and moving memoirs, Anna and Tess recall the extraordinary, and often very difficult, lives they shared with their exceptional parents. Over 50 photos, 344 footnotes, timeline of Campbell's life, and complete index.

MEMOIR

Called to Serve: Life as a Firefighter-Deacon
Deacon Anthony R. Surozenski

Called to Serve is the story of one man's dream to be a firefighter. But dreams have a way of taking detours – so Tony Soruzenski became a teacher and eventually a volunteer firefighter. And when God enters the picture, Tony is faced with a choice. Will he give up firefighting to follow another call? After many years, Tony's two callings are finally united – in service as a fire chaplain at Ground Zero after the 9-11 attacks and in other ways he could not have imagined. Tony is Chief Chaplain's aid for the Massachusettes Corp of Fire Chaplains and Director for the Office of the Diaconate of the Diocese of Worcester, Massachusettes.

HARRY POTTER

The Order of Harry Potter: The Literary Skill of the Hogwarts Epic
Colin Manlove

Colin Manlove, a popular conference speaker and author of over a dozen books, has earned an international reputation as an expert on fantasy and children's literature. His book, *From Alice to Harry Potter*, is a survey of 400 English fantasy books. In *The Order of Harry Potter*, he compares and contrasts *Harry Potter* with works by "Inklings" writers J.R.R. Tolkien, C.S. Lewis and Charles Williams; he also examines Rowling's treatment of the topic of imagination; her skill in organization and the use of language; and the book's underlying motifs and themes.

Harry Potter & Imagination: The Way Between Two Worlds
Travis Prinzi

Imaginative literature places a reader between two worlds: the story world and the world of daily life, and challenges the reader to imagine and to act for a better world. Starting with discussion of Harry Potter's more important themes, *Harry Potter & Imagination* takes readers on a journey through the transformative power of those themes for both the individual and for culture by placing Rowling's series in its literary, historical, and cultural contexts.

Repotting Harry Potter: A Professor's Guide for the Serious Re-Reader
Rowling Revisited: Return Trips to Harry, Fantastic Beasts, Quidditch, & Beedle the Bard
Dr. James W. Thomas

In *Repotting Harry Potter* and his sequel book *Rowling Revisited*, Dr. James W. Thomas points out the humor, puns, foreshadowing and literary parallels in the Potter books. In *Rowling Revisted*, readers will especially find useful three extensive appendixes – "Fantastic Beasts and the Pages Where You'll Find Them," "Quidditch Through the Pages," and "The Books in the Potter Books." Dr. Thomas makes re-reading the Potter books even more rewarding and enjoyable.

Deathly Hallows Lectures:
The Hogwarts Professor Explains Harry's Final Adventure
John Granger

In *The Deathly Hallows Lectures,* John Granger reveals the finale's brilliant details, themes, and meanings. *Harry Potter* fans will be surprised by and delighted with Granger's explanations of the three dimensions of meaning in *Deathly Hallows*. Ms. Rowling has said that alchemy sets the "parameters of magic" in the series; after reading the chapter-length explanation of *Deathly Hallows* as the final stage of the alchemical Great Work, the serious reader will understand how important literary alchemy is in understanding Rowling's artistry and accomplishment.

Hog's Head Conversations: Essays on Harry Potter
Travis Prinzi, Editor

Ten fascinating essays on Harry Potter by popular Potter writers and speakers including John Granger, James W. Thomas, Colin Manlove, and Travis Prinzi.

Sociology and Harry Potter: 22 Enchanting Essays on the Wizarding World
Jenn Simms, editor

Modeled on an Introduction to Sociology textbook, this book is not simply about the series, but also uses the series to facilitate the reader's understanding of the discipline of sociology and a develops a sociological approach to viewing social reality. It is a case of high quality academic scholarship written in a form and on a topic accessible to non-academics. As such, it is written to appeal to Harry Potter fans and the general reading public. Contributors include professional sociologists from eight countries.

Harry Potter, Still Recruiting: An Inner Look at Harry Potter Fandom
Valerie Frankel, editor

The Harry Potter phenomenon has created a new world: one of Quidditch in the park, lightning earrings, endless parodies, a new genre of music, and fan conferences of epic proportions. This book attempts to document everything - exploring costuming, crafting, gaming, and more, with essays and interviews straight from the multitude of creators. From children to adults, fans are delighting the world with an explosion of captivating activities and experiences, all based on Rowling's delightful series.

Unlocking Harry Potter: Five Keys for the Serious Reader
John Granger

"I got so hookede I had to stop everything else I was doing and just read, read, read. I carried it around the house, read it while using the excercycle, I hid in rooms away from the daily life so I could take it all in. A spectacular read for all serious fans of Rowling's works. Compelling, well-argued, fun, and funny. Engaging. Thought provoking. Erudite."

                        Tom Morris
                        author of *If Harry Potter Ran General Electric*
                        Chairman of the Morris Institute for Human Values

Fiction

The Iona Conspiracy (from The Remnant Chronicles book series)
Gary Gregg

Readers find themselves on a modern adventure through ancient Celtic myth and legend as thirteen year old Jacob uncovers his destiny within "the remnant" of the Sporrai Order. As the Iona Academy comes under the control of educational reformers and ideological scientists, Jacob finds himself on a dangerous mission to the sacred Scottish island of Iona and discovers how his life is wrapped up with the fate of the long lost cover of *The Book of Kells*. *Iona* is an adventure that speaks to eternal truths as well as the challenges of the modern world. A young adult novel, *Iona* can be enjoyed by the entire family.

CHRISTIAN LIVING

The Living Word of the Living God:
A Beginner's Guide to Reading and Understanding the Bible
Rev. Tom Furrer

This book is based on over 20 years experience of teaching the Bible to confirmation classes at Episcopal churches in Connecticut. Chapters from Genesis to Revelation.

Keys to Growth: Meditations on the Acts of the Apostles
Will Vaus

Every living thing or person requires certain ingredients in order to grow, and if a thing or person is not growing, it is dying. *The Acts of the Apostles* is a book that is all about growth. Will Vaus has been meditating and preaching on *Acts* for the past 30 years. In this volume, he offers the reader forty-one keys from the entire book of Acts to unlock spiritual growth in everyday life.

Open Before Christmas: Devotional Thoughts For The Holiday Season
Will Vaus

Author Will Vaus seeks to deepen the reader's knowledge of Advent and Christmas leading up to Epiphany. Readers are provided with devotional thoughts for each day that help them to experience this part of the Church Year perhaps in a more spiritually enriching way than ever before.

"Seasoned with inspiring, touching, and sometimes humorous illustrations .... I found his writing immediately engaging and, the more I read, the more I liked it. God has touched my heart by reading Open Before Christmas, and I believe he will touch your heart too."
            The Rev. David Beckmann, Founder of The C.S. Lewis Society of Chattanooga

God's Love Letter: Reflections on I John
Will Vaus

Various words for "love" appear thirty-five times in the five brief chapters of I John. This book invites you on a journey of reading and reflection: reading this book in the New Testament and reflecting on God's love for us, our love for God, and our love for one another.

Jogging with G.K. Chsterton: 65 Earthshaking Expeditions
Robert Moore-Jumonville

Jogging with G.K. Chesterton is a showcase for the merry mind of Chesterton. But Chesterton's lighthearted wit always runs side-by-side with his weighty wisdom. These 65 "earthshaking expeditions" will keep you smiling and thinking from start to finish. You'll be entertained, challenged, and spiritually uplifted as you take time to breath in the fresh morning air and contemplate the wonders of the world.

"This is a delightfully improbable book in which Chesterton puts us through our spiritual and intellectual exercises."
            Joseph Pearce, author of *Wisdom and Innocence: A Life of G.K. Chesterton*

www.ingramcontent.com/pod-product-compliance
Lightning Source LLC
Chambersburg PA
CBHW020414080526
44584CB00014B/1317